*Twayne's United States Authors Series*

EDITOR OF THIS VOLUME

Sylvia E. Bowman

*Indiana University*

*William Graham Sumner*

TUSAS 391

William Graham Sumner

# WILLIAM GRAHAM SUMNER

### By BRUCE CURTIS
*Michigan State University*

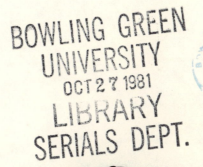

## TWAYNE PUBLISHERS
### A DIVISION OF G. K. HALL & CO., BOSTON

Published in 1981 by Twayne Publishers,
A Division of G. K. Hall & Co.
All Rights Reserved

Printed on permanent/durable acid-free paper and bound
in the United States of America

*First Printing*

**Library of Congress Cataloging in Publication Data**

Curtis, Bruce.
William Graham Sumner.

(Twayne's United States authors series ; TUSAS 391)
Bibliography: p. 178–82
Includes index.
1. Sociology—United States—History.
2. Sumner, William Graham, 1840–1910. I. Title.
II. Series.
HM22.U6S82          301'.092'4 [B]          81-1137
ISBN 0-8057-7324-X          AACR2

To my mother,
Josephine Teeter Curtis,
and to the memory of my father,
Chester Kerlin Curtis

# Contents

# About the Author

Bruce E. Curtis was born, reared, and educated in Iowa. After being awarded a Parsons College B.A. in 1955, and then serving in the army, he studied American Intellectual History at the University of Iowa, where he received the Ph.D. in 1964. His dissertation, which established his interest in the subject of this book, was a study of "The Middle-Class Progressivism of William Graham Sumner."

He taught at the University of Wichita and at Kansas State College of Pittsburg before joining the faculty of the Department of American Thought and Language at Michigan State University in 1965, where he is now a professor. He has also served as a visiting professor in James Madison and Justin Morrill Colleges, residential schools in Michigan State University. Professor Curtis has published articles on Sumner in *Mid-America, American Studies*, the *New England Quarterly*, and the *Journal of American History*, as well as a number of reviews in the latter journal. His articles, reviews, and poems have also appeared in various journals and little magazines, including *University College Quarterly, Communities, Communitas, Beggar's Bowl*, and *Star-Web Paper*.

In addition to having a continuing interest in American thought between the Civil War and World War I and a developing interest in the history of women, Professor Curtis is especially interested in comparing Utopian and Communitarian ideas and experimentation in America with similar manifestations in other cultures. Having learned that even William Graham Sumner was a Utopian, he is firmly convinced that Utopianism offers an interpretive key to much of American thought and experience.

# *Preface*

William Graham Sumner's career extended from 1870, when he took an Episcopal pastorate, to 1909, when he retired after long and distinguished service as a professor at Yale and as one of America's pioneering sociologists. In the intervening years, Sumner also worked as an economist, political scientist, historian, educator, and public servant. In each capacity, he was a public speaker, scholar, and writer. But today, when not confused with the Civil War senator from Massachusetts, Sumner is remembered chiefly as the author of *Folkways* or as the social Darwinist spokesman for conservative causes.

In an attempt to deal with Sumner as a whole man, this book focuses on a substratum of ideas and loyalties that informed all of his thought and writing. It examines the disciplines and interests that Sumner followed, but it does so primarily to mark his perennial search for the truth and the harmony that, he believed, existed under the apparent disorder of life. Consequently, the structure of this work is broadly chronological, with topical chapters that address subjects important for his developing world view as he moved from pulpit to professorship, from Theism to Naturalism, and from a hopeful to a somber, pessimistic mood concerning prospects for American and human life generally.

In an era whose overriding social and intellectual ferment challenged all faiths and assumptions, Sumner doggedly sought to find and integrate truths. And then he wished to express them in any of several fields in his desire to serve his fellow men. As a servant, Sumner was an elitist leader whose loyalties were to the methods of modern science and to middle-class, capitalistic, and, with appropriate reservations, democratic society. This study, then, attempts to assess Sumner's contributions both as an engaged public servant and critic and as a man of thought and letters. It finds not only that Sumner made important contributions in both spheres but also that perhaps his significance derived less from specific acts and ideas than from the qualities of mind and character he exhibited in his search for truth.

In a business extending over several years, I have contracted many debts. Stow Persons guided my preparation of a Sumner dissertation. I have been helped by librarians of Brown, Columbia, Harvard, and Michigan State universities; the universities of Iowa and Wisconsin; the Library of Congress; the New York Public Library; the United States Naval Academy; and the County Records Office, Preston, England. The librarians of Yale University, particularly Judith Schiff, Howard B. Gotlieb, and Jane W. Hill, offered indispensable aid. I especially thank Janet Camp Troxell, Deane Keller, and John Chamberlain for useful information and access to Sumner material. Reed Baird, Philip Korth, and James McClintock read the manuscript, repeatedly saving me from mistakes and infelicity. Errors are mine. Michigan State University tendered several All University Research Grants. I must thank, most of all, Joy Hilleary Curtis for contributions that writers with the good fortune to have mates of quick intelligence and ready sympathy can appreciate. Finally, my thanks to Hilary and Jason, who also served.

BRUCE CURTIS

*Irons, Michigan*
*East Lansing, Michigan*

# Chronology

1840    William Graham Sumner born in Paterson, New Jersey, on October 30.

1859    Matriculates at Yale College.

1863    Graduates from Yale. Studies theology, languages, and scientific method at Geneva, Göttingen, and Oxford.

1866    Returns to Yale as tutor.

1867    Is ordained Deacon in Episcopal Church while continuing as tutor.

1869    Leaves tutoring in March upon being named assistant to the rector of Calvary Church, New York City, and the editor of the *Living Church*. Is ordained as priest in July.

1870    Becomes rector of the Church of the Redeemer, Morristown, New Jersey, in September.

1871    Marries Jeannie Elliott, April 17.

1872    Assumes duties in chair of political and social science at Yale in September. Publishes translated edition of K. C. W. F. Bähr's, *The Books of the Kings, Book 2*.

1873    Is elected as Republican New Haven alderman.

1874    *A History of American Currency*.

1875    Is converted to evolution. Offers "sociology" course for the first time.

1876    Is member of Democratic party national committee delegation sent to Louisiana to investigate disputed presidential election. Fails to be reelected as alderman.

1877    *Lectures on the History of Protection in the United States*.

1879    Is drawn into academic-freedom controversy over use of Herbert Spencer's *Study of Sociology* as a text.

1882    *Andrew Jackson as a Public Man*.

1883    *What Social Classes Owe to Each Other*. Becomes member of Connecticut State Board of Education and continues until his death.

1885    *Protectionism: The -Ism Which Teaches That Waste Makes Wealth. Collected Essays in Political and Social Science*.

1890    Breaks down in health. *Alexander Hamilton*.

1891    Two-volume study of Robert Morris, *The Financier and the Finances of the American Revolution.*

1892    *Robert Morris.*

1896    *History of Banking in the United States.*

1899    Gives "The Conquest of the United States by Spain" before Yale Phi Beta Kappa Society on January 16.

1906    *Folkways.*

1909    Upon retirement is awarded an honorary Doctorate of Laws by Yale University. Is named President of American Sociological Society. Suffers stroke, December 26.

1910    Dies, April 12.

1911-   *War and Other Essays, Earth-Hunger and Other Essays,*
1919    *The Challenge of Facts and Other Essays,* and *The Forgotten Man and Other Essays* (with bibliography) are edited and published by Albert Galloway Keller.

1927    *The Science of Society,* in four volumes, is completed by Keller and published under the coauthorship of Sumner and Keller.

# CHAPTER 1

# *Preparation*

W HEN William Graham Sumner, born in 1840, retired in 1909 after thirty-seven years at Yale University as a professor of political and social science, an admiring former student described the scene when Sumner was awarded an honorary doctoral degree in law:

You should have seen Sumner get his degree! . . . A simply terrific hand clapping burst out, the young fellows and old ones yelled and cheered, men waved hats even. The old gentleman was much confused. He isn't good on his pins and he kind of staggered out . . . and stood there bowed over a little, letting the hurricane of cheers clatter about his bald head—his last earthly recognition, I guess it was. It was fine, yet pitiful. . . . Then sudden quiet. . . . [William Lyon] Phelps read a few words. Then he said, reading, *"always a radical."* At that word the old man . . . straightened his shoulders back like a shot. . . . The audience roared aloud with delight, actually yelled. It was so characteristic of Sumner! . . . Phelps said something about Yale's "great progress." Sumner heard it and . . . pulled his nose with a nervous jerk and the audience yelled again. Sumner must have caught on . . . that he was the same man . . . that he was all his life. . . . straightening his back at the word "radical" and pulling his nose at "progress." . . . [Arthur Twining] Hadley confirmed the degree and Sumner turned to get another yell that lasted all the way to his seat and for minutes afterward.[1]

William Graham Sumner's public life exemplifies the American success myth. Born of humble parents, themselves of humble ancestry, he retired in a hailstorm of cheers from his colleagues, friends, and former students who included President William Howard Taft. A great university had taken the unusual step of awarding one of its own graduates, teachers, and major scholars an honorary doctorate of laws. Sumner's success story reflects the conjunction of an internalized work ethic and fortunate conditions; but, less obviously and publicly, his life was devoted to a search. In an

13

industrializing, urbanizing, and immigrant society, in an era of
rapid and unsettling intellectual change, he sought stability, certainty, and harmony in society and even in the universe. That his
quest for certainty, even for the certainty of a law of change, was
markedly less successful than his professional accomplishments only
makes Sumner representative of a great many Americans of his era.

## I   *Ancestry and Family*

Sumner's English ancestry was from Walton-le-Dale in Lancashire.[2] Having no obviously distinguished forebears, Sumner knew
only that they had long been workers and craftsmen—yeomen,
weavers, block cutters, print cutters. The name of Sumner did not,
it seems, appear on the lists of charities; but in the England of 1836
the family's tradition of independence and self-reliance must have
seemed threatened to William Graham Sumner's father, Thomas
Sumner, who was then twenty-eight years old, poorly educated but
ambitious, and financially hard pressed. Economic uncertainty and
hardship were endemic in the post-Napoleonic era, especially as the
factory-machine system overwhelmed Lancashire's peasant and
craft society. Instead of taking charity, Thomas Sumner turned for
relief to America, which was soon absorbed in its own industrial
revolution but whose prospects seemed bright to millions of nineteenth-century European emigrants. Thomas Sumner eventually
settled at the symbolic center of that revolution, as a railroad shop
mechanic, in Hartford, Connecticut.

But he was not satisfied to remain merely a wage earner at
perhaps twenty dollars a week. If he had so remained, his son's life
would have been significantly different; for no other person influenced the development of William Graham Sumner's character
more than his father. The ambition that moved Thomas Sumner to
emigrate drove him to better himself educationally, economically,
and, always, morally. He was the classic nineteenth-century, self-
educated workingman who, alone or in "mechanic's institutes,"
studied public matters and religious questions. Attempting to become an entrepreneur in his later years, he managed the housing
property of others; and then, with tediously saved and borrowed
capital, he turned to building houses. That Thomas Sumner failed
to become wealthy, indeed died poor, was not important. It was
important to his son, however, that Thomas Sumner practiced as
well as preached the industrial virtues of abstinence, honesty, and
hard work. In later years, Sumner referred to his father as "a man of

the strictest integrity, a total abstainer, of domestic habits and indefatigable industry." [3]

When William Graham Sumner wrote, while studying in Europe, that he wished to try Germany, his orthodox Episcopalian father replied, "I should regret exceedingly if you should come back a confirmed German skeptic. . . . Apply your own rule as you applied it to the Universalist church when I asked you about going one Sunday night. You then thought it best to avoid any place of doubtful reputation." [4] And later, as a young minister and editor of a church journal, Sumner highly valued his father's opinion of his sermons and writings. [5] When he characterized his father as independent, self-reliant, honest, abstinent, moral, self-educated, hard-working, and commonsensical, Sumner seems to have done so with reasonable accuracy. Thomas Sumner's detractors, if he had any, might have said, as his son's opponents later believed of him, that he was dogmatic, hardheaded, undemonstrative.

Little is known about Sumner's mother, Sarah Graham, except that her parents had emigrated from Lancashire and that her father, whose character and allegiance to the ethic of work apparently resembled Thomas Sumner's, was a small farmer and locksmith who dabbled in astronomy. After she died in 1848 when William was eight and one of three young children, Thomas Sumner soon married Eliza Van Alstein, who evidently took the family under her management but not under her wing. Although William Graham Sumner said he hated her and, with his younger brother, plotted to murder her, he later appreciated both her insistence that he attend college and her thrift that made doing so possible. Somehow his parents managed to draw together a college fund of approximately $1,000, perhaps a year's wages in the railroad shops. Not long after Sumner's stepmother died early in 1859, Thomas Sumner married Catherine Mix, whom he described as a "good Samaritan." William grew fond of her; and, following his father's death, she often lived with him. But Kate Mix apparently had little formative influence upon him.

## II  *Education*

When Sumner matriculated at Yale College in 1859, he was a graduate of his father's house—and his stepmother's—and of the common schools of Hartford, Connecticut. Although he admired certain Hartford teachers for their honesty, candor, and teaching ability, his most significant early intellectual experience was gained independently. When thirteen or fourteen, he found in the library of Hartford's Young Men's Institute, Harriet Martineau's *Illustrations of Political Economy*. He learned from such little books prescriptions of laissez-faire and free-trade economics that admirably complemented the home truths he had absorbed. Years later Sumner believed that "my conceptions of capital, labor, money, and trade, were all formed by those books which I read in my boyhood."[6] In his boyhood, Sumner also began to develop a command of writing that later enabled him to compose a mass of material even while performing onerous research and teaching tasks. The few manuscripts that survive from Sumner's boyhood are written in clear, workmanlike prose; and the narratives reveal an attraction to romantic adventure stories. As a youth, he continued to write occasional stories and even imagined himself as a poet; but poetry and fiction, even fiction with a moral, were for a scholar's idle times; and Sumner revealed his literary interests to few friends.

When young Will Sumner arrived at Yale, he was equipped not only with the basic educational tools but with a purpose. The serious-mindedness that his home life had inculcated had been given special direction by the Reverend Elias Beadle, a scholarly Hartford minister. Under his influence, Sumner had left his father's church to become a Congregationalist and, eventually, a minister. He had also returned to high school from an unrewarding job to prepare for college. Young Sumner would become, as he later wrote, the first in his family line to learn Latin and algebra; and, whether as a minister or as an academic, he would devote his life to converting his fellow man to his beliefs.

Yale in 1859 fitted neatly the earnest young Sumner's cultural and intellectual profile. Observers remarked that "Yale was a thoroughly conservative institution: traditional in its habits, religious in its spirit, earnest and moral in its atmosphere, conforming in its opinions, old-fashioned in its education."[7] Many years later, the publisher Henry Holt of the class of 1862 remembered his alma mater as "probably at its very worst in mind, body, and estate. In mind it dated back centuries. . . . The training in the classics was almost all in the grammar, and while we were studying chemistry they actually gave us a pamphlet of chemical formulas to learn by heart."[8] The curriculum of the first three years was almost entirely prescribed—Latin, Greek, mathematics, and rhetoric; but juniors could also choose a modern language or mineralogy. By comparison, the courses for seniors formed a potpourri, even if prescribed and superficial, of history, theology, astronomy, chemistry, the American Constitution, moral and political philosophy, and the history of philosophy.

Most students probably expected little else from formal education in a mid-nineteenth-century college, but any discontentment about the narrow curriculum must have been allayed by the intensive extracurricular life that combined social and educational purposes. Sumner, who wholeheartedly participated in Yale's clubs and societies, emerged at graduation as a highly honored writer, orator, debater, and eating-club member. He was first in the freshman, sophomore, and senior debates of the "Brothers" society; and he served in three of its offices, including the presidency. He tied for first place in sophomore English composition with his friend William C. Whitney; and he was third to Whitney's first in declamation. He was a junior class orator, and he was elected to Psi Upsilon, a junior society; to Phi Beta Kappa; and, most importantly, to the club called "Skull and Bones." In the long years following graduation, members were accustomed to refer to and favor one another as "Bones men." In addition to these honors, Sumner won as a senior one of five awards for composition. Despite a busy extracurricular life, he graduated eighth in a class of 122.

And Bill Sumner emerged with friends. Reserved, even cold in appearance, harsh and open in judging others, Sumner nevertheless made a small number of loyal, well-to-do friends who were important to his future well-being and advancement. Preeminent among these was his rival in composition and declamation, William C. Whitney. Another lifelong friend, Frederick Kernochan, wrote of Sumner at Yale, "I came to know that the New England reserve was only skin deep and to his intimates he was always warm-hearted and genial."[9] But, to those not among his intimates, Sumner was an irritant. When the incubating young minister visited Hartford, "invariably dressed in dark clothing, his countenance as somber as his raiment, impertinent youngsters would sometimes cry after him, 'Mister, why don't you smile?'"[10] Perhaps those youngsters smarted from their feeling that Sumner, always self-centered and morally righteous, had affected aristocratic and dandified airs. He admitted later to being a "pronounced defender of aristocracy and monarchy" in college.[11] Surely Yale, its associations and honors, weighed heavily with a mechanic's son. In 1909 Sumner remembered of his Yale entrance paper that "no diploma any king or potentate could give would seem so great."[12] For the ambitious young nineteenth-century man, college training led to membership in a social and intellectual elite.[13]

### III    *European Study*

But, since not even Yale sufficed for the person who wished the best modern ministerial training, Sumner, like many of his contemporaries, pursued graduate work in Europe. For this sojourn his father's resources were inadequate, particularly since a Civil War substitute had had to be procured and paid to replace the recently drafted William. But financial aid from his friends, his father, and his brother made the venture in Europe possible. William C. Whitney, who was Sumner's chief benefactor, prevailed upon his older brother, Henry M. Whitney, to advance a sum and to pay for the substitute in the army. Other friends and classmates, among them Frederick Kernochan and Henry Dimock, also lent Sumner money for study in Europe; but over the years these loans tended to become gifts. Kernochan, who held the note for Sumner's debt, asked in 1874 if William C. Whitney or Henry M. Whitney could "take $500 of the old Bill Sumner matter"; for several thousands of dollars remained to be paid by Sumner who could never do so.[14]

Surely Sumner's dedication to learning repaid his friends' investment. Without waiting for Yale's graduation day, Sumner sailed for Europe after a farewell dinner with Whitney at New York's fashionable Delmonico's. On the long voyage, during which he studied the passengers, French, and sailing, Sumner wrote his father that he meant to learn "about anything and everything I can."[15] By October 1863, after touring Britain, he was settled as an English tutor with a family in Geneva. While in Geneva, Sumner occasionally attended university lectures on religion; but he concentrated on the private study of French and Hebrew. His journal testifies that he spent long hours learning the verbs perfectly, conning word lists, and reading church history. On Christmas Day, 1863, when Sumner studied French for six hours, he perhaps established, perhaps maintained, a tradition of working virtually every day. Almost his only recreation was taking walks.

Sumner soon concluded that, compared to the German universities, Geneva was inadequate. Despite both his father's warnings and the milder cautionings of the Reverend Elias Beadle about the dangers of German skepticism, he moved to the University of Göttingen for a two-year stay. There he continued Hebrew; perfected German; studied Old Testament criticism, history, and theology; exercised little; and worked incessantly. Until William C. Whitney and Sumner's father and brother supplied more funds, Sumner's fears that he would be unable to stay contributed to several illnesses and to mental depression. But he persevered because he realized that such a chance would not recur. "Think only of what you will be if you are strong," he told himself, "and that which you will not be if you are weak. . . . I think of that which is in the future and I have patience and hope." [16]

Sumner survived the scholar's ordeal and saw his hopes realized. Twenty-five years later he recalled that he had "enjoyed intensely" working at Göttingen, where the professors of "biblical science" were "bent on seeking a clear and comprehensive conception of the matter under study. . . . They . . . taught me rigorous and pitiless methods of investigation and deduction." [17] Even while he was still in Europe, he wrote to Dr. Beadle that "Göttingen is the only place at which I have yet studied which satisfied me. The thoroughness of their scholarship and the scientific accuracy of their methods are unrivaled. I shall rejoice all my life long that it has been my privilege to study there." [18]

Nevertheless, Sumner had begun to feel out of touch with Anglo-American theology. He left Göttingen in April 1866; and, after touring on the Continent, he was reading in the Bodleian Library of Oxford University by late May. But he found English theological scholarship disappointing because it was too dependent on either outdated or reworked German studies. Like many young nine-teenth-century American scholars, Sumner had been "thoroughly Teutonized"; [19] and a few years later, in 1870, he was still very much the Germanophile. Although determined to settle as a happy and useful citizen and husband, he confessed to his fiancée, Jeannie Elliott, that, formerly, "If I had any great hope for the future, it was that I might some day go back to Germany and become a great scholar. That dream has always clung to me dimly." [20]

In England, only Richard Hooker's *Of the Laws of Ecclesiastical Polity* seemed important to Sumner. Hooker's discussion of church and civil polity fitted perfectly Sumner's preconceptions concerning constitutional order and authority and historical continuity. More-over, Hooker's work renewed his interest in political science, and his reading of Henry Thomas Buckle's *History of Civilization in England* intensified that interest. Sumner and like-minded Oxonians discussed at length Buckle's attempt to establish the laws of history and the related question as to whether or not a science of society was possible. They agreed that a social science had to be derived from historical knowledge, but they also recognized the difficulty of gathering the mass of historical material into usable form. Sumner later remarked that, of the Oxford group, only he had become a social scientist. In view of his later attitudes and professional development, the significance of his European experience centered not so much on religious content as upon scientific method.

The experience abroad was also important because it gave Sumner a tantalizing taste of the aristocratic life for which he sometimes hungered. Oxford, he later said, was pleasant if one had an income, so that "one could be a gentleman and not worry over the other poor cusses who were working along."[21] In Europe, he met the Duke of Argyle's son, Lord Archibald Campbell; toured Scotland with him; and consequently met other persons of rank. Sumner later wrote to "Campbell," with whom he developed a lifelong friendship, to congratulate him for taking a bank position and to comment that "I am not one of those who think that hereditary rank is 'played out.' It will last, at least in England, for a long time yet, but in the future, those families and those persons who are careful to ally rank with successful achievement . . . will be the only ones which will retain their preeminence."[22] Characteristically, Sumner was drawn to elegance, refinement, and rank, as well as to a man's duty to be socially useful.

Although an immigrant's son, Sumner was never a displaced person socially, primarily because his English heritage translated easily into American terms. Yet his terrible urge to know and to succeed, which was more sharpened than satiated by his Yale and his European studies, made him another kind of marginal man in his society and ensured that he would hardly ever be certain whether he should be an American or a European: he had dreamed dreams of becoming a great German scholar. "A statesman, scientist, philosopher, artist," wrote Sumner early in the twentieth century, "can win far greater distinction before the world if he lives in Europe than . . . in America."[23] Characteristically, in later years Sumner did not take a train to the American Rockies to restore his health and soothe his spirit; he boarded a ship to Europe and the Alps.

In June 1866, on the recommendation of a friend—and no doubt for his own scholarly reputation—Sumner was named tutor in Yale College, a position that called for classroom teaching as well as tutoring. Since he was unaware of being proposed and considered, he received the news of the honor with mixed feelings because he had planned either to visit Egypt and Palestine or to return to America and the ministry. He did, however, welcome the opportunity to continue studying about the American church system before taking a pastorate. Nonetheless, his acceptance letter expressed unwillingness to leave unused for longer than a year his expensive education in theology. Sumner's question as to what he was to teach suggests that the young European scholar did not feel at all incompetent to tutor. But, when the mechanic's son returned from Geneva and Göttingen and Oxford to the Yale that seven years earlier had been so awe-inspiring, he felt somewhat lowered in the scholarly world as he sat in the "tutors' box" in Old Chapel.

## IV  *Character and Personality*

There is no telling precisely what forms a man's character and personality, but for Sumner certain influences seem preeminent; and the most important of these were the personality and ethic of his father, whose strength and independence were fused with a moralistic and virtually religious adherence to abstinence, honesty, and hard work. Moreover, William Sumner's early unsettled home situation, including his mother's death and his stepmother's character, as well as the family's straitened economic circumstances, affected him fundamentally. Sumner grew up poor in a society that urged and rewarded upward mobility in many obvious and subtle ways. With a drive and an ethic similar to his father's and in a society that offered opportunities for success—business, for wealth; law, for the public minded; the ministry and college teaching, for the scholarly—Sumner was a logical candidate for success. But such logic depended partly on chance for fruition: that one of the great locomotive wheels that Thomas Sumner machined back into round did not fall and crush him; that for his second wife he married a good manager; that Dr. Beadle took an interest in Sumner, who responded. Had these conditions been different, Sumner, given his considerable talents, might well have made his own way, but the way would have been different. As it was, his family provided funds; and he went to Yale best prepared to emulate certain models—teachers and preachers. There, and in Europe, he associated with an abundance of both; and both pointed him toward the scholarly life.

To this life his personality also inclined him. Young Sumner did not get on well and easily with people; he could not or would not meet them on jovial and democratic terms; he dressed and walked with dignified air; he avoided sports and strenuous exercise; he found his rewards in lonely reading and classroom competition; and he moralized to his peers, even to his elders. In short, he was a prig. Maturation, college life, some worldly experience, and the recognition that those he met could help or hinder his chances taught an older Sumner to conceal certain of the more abrasive aspects of his personality; but, even as a public person, he did not change fundamentally.

Privately, especially with friends and those he loved, Sumner revealed his warmer self. In 1870, at the age of thirty, he fell in love with Jeannie Elliott, an utterly charming New York City merchant's daughter with a quick mind and a ready pen. In Sumner's letters during their courtship, he revealed his sense of self—personality, character, ambitions—as he never had, or would, to anyone else. At thirty, in love and often still awake "under the midnight gas" after a long day's study, Sumner viewed himself as lonely and reserved, perhaps as even cold and hard: "I suppose I am, or was. Why should I not be? I lived for years almost entirely alone. Sometimes I passed whole days without speaking a word to anybody—not because I was morose but because I did not have occasion or opportunity. But I assure you that I am not incapable of tenderness and affection."[24] Sumner revealed to Jeannie that as a minister he studied small talk but that he disliked calling on parishioners; for he much preferred people—such as Jeannie Elliott—who shared common interests and understood him. He liked associating with equals, he told Jeannie, " 'dignified men' and I assure you that I am rarely frightened or overpowered."[25] He saw himself as a natural leader who was "with the select minority against the crowd. I am quite used to finding myself there. I do not put on any airs about it . . . but I understand my position perfectly and . . . that of those who disagree with me far better than they do themselves so I am satisfied."[26]

Especially evident in Sumner's letters to Jeannie were his concerns with his and their social class position, his financial plans for the two of them, and his expectation that Jeannie would help him subordinate his personal ambition to his duty to society. Although he was not ashamed of his parents, Sumner told Jeannie, he had risen above them socially. Yet, when Edgar Wells had paid court to Jeannie, Sumner had envied young Wells because he was the son of the Secretary of the Navy. Perhaps because of his humble background, Sumner informed his fiancée that he had dined with the E. L. Godkins of the public affairs journal, the *Nation,* and that he was "glad that they take so much interest in me and mine."[27] Sumner was critical of the fast summer set at Long Branch, New Jersey, whom he called those "horse and theater" people—people who included even the President's family. America badly needed a "social center," but who could expect the unsophisticated Ulysses S. Grant family to provide that? Much more preferable to Sumner was the society of Morristown, New Jersey, where he was taking up a pastorate in 1870 after being ordained in 1869: "The town is old and *very aristocratic*. I never heard so much stress laid upon this point anywhere else. The congregation is composed of a little clique of this class of people. I liked all of them whom I met very much indeed. They were very polite and well-bred."[28]

Sumner claimed he had never worried about money; but in 1870, when he and Jeannie were soon to be married, he was much concerned that they would have enough to avoid worries and to save even a small amount, as he was accustomed to do. It was shameful, he wrote to Jeannie, that neither preaching nor teaching paid well, and it was sad that he would have no inheritance; but, as they both knew, Jeannie had a modest income, she would be a good manager, and he had just been paid his first money for a publication, an article in the *Nation*. Perhaps their combined incomes would reach twenty-four hundred dollars; thus he wrote Jeannie, "I can live on 1200 [*sic*] if you can."[29]

Money was necessary, but it was not a prime object, Sumner told Jeannie; neither was worldly success. The young minister-scholar, ambitious yet ambivalent, asserted that "I will not give way to . . . weakness if I can help it and I want you to help me. You have ambition for me, but you must take care, darling, that your ambition is for me to do all my duty to *the best of my ability*, and not that I should win reputation and success. I want you to be a *conscience* to me and keep me right."[30]

In her letters, Jeannie Elliott drew out and mirrored Sumner's earnestness; but she encouraged and enjoyed his lighter side as well by teasing him about their engagement that had cost her fiancé his influence with the girls in his parish and by teasing him with such nicknames as "Graham" and "Graeme." Sumner was bewitched by Jeannie and revealed that he had nothing against dancing but that he deferred to "popular prejudice" against such frivolity because he was a clergyman. He also revealed to Jeannie that she awakened the "sentiment and romance" in him and that he eagerly anticipated a fortnight at the shore with her and a chaperone.[31]

Sumner was drawn to sentiment and romance, but these he took seriously; and he sometimes played croquet with the ladies, but he played to win. The point is that Sumner was rarely able to submerge or escape from his serious self. Two examples may illustrate the point. After Sumner moved to Morristown, but before his books arrived, he wrote to his fiancée that loafing made him miserable and that "I want all sorts of things. I want you and inasmuch as I cannot have you yet I suppose that it would be well for me to forget the wants and I cannot do that without my books."[32] Lonely, deprived of both his loves, he hardly knew which he wanted more. Those of Sumner's friends who knew of his love affair with books and his former determined advocacy of bachelorhood were surprised to learn of his engagement to marry. One friend wrote that surely Sumner read to his fiancée from Hegel and Kant rather than from Longfellow and Mrs. Browning and that she must wear spectacles and write for the *North American Review*. Sumner's friend was wrong about Jeannie, but he was implicitly right about Sumner, who sent the *Nation* to his true love.

# CHAPTER 2

## Changing Religious Views

THE bald contrast between Sumner's later attitude to religion and his early expressions and works of faith is startling. In his later days Sumner wrote that "all the men who know something and have some training are agnostics about history, ethics, philosophy and religion and are slow to act. All the men who do not know . . . are hot and eager mattoids with fads."[1] In *Folkways*, his great sociological study published in 1906, he declared, "If there are any superior powers which meddle with history, it is certain that men have never yet found out how their ways and human ways react on each other, nor any means of interpreting their ways."[2] By the late nineteenth century, experience and study had convinced Sumner that realism demanded, if not unbelief, at least an agnostic attitude to religion. Anthropology taught that religion grew from the savage's need to propitiate the forces that determined his luck and pointed his destiny. But, to a scientific man, religion was a "fantasm." So far as Sumner knew, man, like other animals, was without supernatural guidance or perhaps without even a moral sense. Man alone, as an end to himself, had to find meaning in self-realization.[3]

Despite his reputation as a critic of sham and delusion, Sumner was no magnified village skeptic like his famous agnostic contemporary, Robert Green Ingersoll. Ingersoll, Sumner told students, did "a very pernicious thing" by breaking down a traditional moral system before a new one was available to replace it.[4] But as a social scientist Sumner welcomed the modern decline of religion and the rise of toleration. To him, superstition and dogmatism had "traversed" the struggle for existence by wasting capital; by impeding the growth of rational, scientific knowledge; and by inciting ethnocentric wars when mankind's true hope was in "harmonious cooperation." Religion had no doubt contributed by promoting sanitary and hygienic practices, by supporting monogamy, and by promising future rewards for present hard times; and it had thereby served as

25

an instrument of social control. Christian ethics had had some minor positive influence in two thousand years, as when it had advocated emancipating slaves. But its wastefulness of wealth, its opposition to usury, its suppression of free thought, and its sectarian struggles that often led to war presented a "frightful indictment" against Christianity and religion generally.[5]

## I  *Early Religious Views*

Although Sumner told students that he and his brother as boys awoke on Sunday mornings to "condole with each other" at the prospect of a dull day, he also told one of his sons that he had always wanted to preach.[6] Perhaps different audiences inspired different memories, but Sumner was undoubtedly a seriously religious young man. Influenced by his religiously and ethically minded father and by the Reverend Elias Beadle, he took one of the traditional American routes of sincere and ambitious young men to respectability and prestige—the ministry.

The Protestant clergyman's central responsibility was the sermon. Sumner began as an adolescent to practice, perhaps to preach, by drafting several sermons that revealed an orthodox Congregational theology expressed in terms at least mildly evangelical, as the following excerpt suggests: " 'Freely ye have received, freely give.' Yes, indeed, freely have ye received! All those blessings God has showered down upon you, my Christian friend, and you must give an account of their use. He has given you them and you may have thought they were very bountiful and have thanked him for them; but, Oh! have you remembered the accompanying duty to extend them to others. The Lord gave you the blessings, but he also gave you the duties."[7]

As late as 1864, at Geneva while he was under stress and lonely, Sumner revealed emotional and romantic aspects of his religious outlook:

Dimanche le 28 Feb. I have just read over the letter that Hattie Morgan wrote me. . . . I think of her nearly every day. . . . A year ago today she wrote me these lines and now she is in her grave and I am nearly four thousand miles away. Even while I write at ten at night the February sun is setting on her grave or perhaps the wintry storms are beating on it. . . . I know, however, that she is not there. . . . If the redeemed see each other she is with my mother and there are two at least in that upper world who love me. . . . What is in the future for me I do not know. God knows. His providence has worked upon me so wonderfully that I cannot but leave myself to Him for the future.[8]

## II    *Maturing Religious Views*

But Sumner only rarely expressed himself in this emotional fashion. As he matured, especially under the impact of German training, the Romantic tendency withered; and he treated religion in increasingly "scientific," professional terms. Apparently noting Sumner's development, William C. Whitney hoped that he would not fall into atheism; "but I don't care what a man believes if he has come to it honestly, and we are waiting to pin ourselves on to your coattails."[9] Sumner's friends were not only interested in his theological views but intensified the pressure Sumner felt to prepare himself fully. Because of their friendly influence and because of his study and personal inclination, he came to regret his boyhood conversion to Congregationalism. In 1865 Bill Whitney wrote to Sumner for himself and for "Dim" and Charley Wesson that "We are all of us Episcopalians, Bill, and you must be the same, can't you? I don't mean to say do it because we are, but don't you like it best? . . . The Episcopal Church is undoubtedly taking the best classes of society here and I think for the good reason that there is less to offend enlightened feelings in it."[10]

In June 1866 Sumner wrote to Dr. Beadle that he had joined Beadle's church from personal affection but had been too young to know his mind. He had soon learned at Yale, however, that he preferred Episcopal to Calvinist theology; and his European training had strengthened that preference. As for his reasons, Sumner believed they were not doctrinal ones; to him the Episcopal hierarchy was "convenient," and its ceremonies were unobjectionable. Conversely, he disliked emotional prayer meetings: "I could not bear to lead one . . . and hear such bad taste and bad theology as one sometimes hears. . . . I do not like the doctrine of conversion as it is commonly taught. I say nothing of predestination because I believe that it is not now held by our American churches, at least in its rigor." Sumner, who hoped he would not appear fickle, especially to his father, closed his letter with remarks about the "orderings of Providence" that had directed his life.[11] In 1863 Sumner had gone to Europe a Congregationalist slightly tinged with Romantic enthusiasm; in 1866 he returned as a biblical scientist to America and to the Episcopal Church of his father and of his friends, of Bill Whitney, Henry Dimock, and Charley Wesson.

While tutoring, Sumner continued his religious apprenticeship by directing the Sunday School at Trinity Episcopal Church. The pastor, Dr. Edwin Harwood, a liberal who was receptive to biblical criticism and the new science, appealed to Sumner. But he began to doubt the wisdom of entering the ministry. He later described an experience common to Americans with German religious training: "I speedily found that there was no demand at all for 'biblical science'; that everybody was afraid of it, especially if it came with the German label on it. It was a case in which, if a man should work very hard and achieve remarkable results, the only consequence would be that he would ruin himself." [12] Although Sumner had earlier refused to be committed beyond a year of tutoring, he now extended that work to a second and then to a third year. Nevertheless, he was ordained deacon in 1867 and, through Dr. Harwood's influence, received the task of translating and editing K. C. W. F. Bähr's *The Books of the Kings, Book Two.*

### III    Living Church *Editor*

In 1869 Sumner was called to assist Harwood's friend, the Reverend E.A. Washburn, rector of Calvary Church, New York City; but his chief task was to edit a new monthly, the *Living Church*, which several "broad" Episcopal clergymen had established to "find harmony between Revelation and science . . . meet the practical and social problems of Christianity at this day, and prove the reality of the Kingdom of God in its work." [13] Apparently, however, interest in a high-level journal was too much confined to a small elite of clergy and laymen, for the *Living Church* died after a year and a dozen issues.

While it lived, this publication was virtually a reflection of its editor's interests; it showed the impress of biblical science and the *Nation*, and it called for a reinvigoration of the church's spiritual and intellectual life. The state of the Episcopal Church seemed dismal to Sumner, split as it was among the "high," the "low," and the "broad" churchmen with whom he identified himself. He was not a "low," he told his fiancée, because that group was evangelistic in temper, "Calvinistic in doctrine and Methodistical in behavior. I am a great deal too sincere a churchman to like that. If I wanted Calvinism I would go where they have it." He was not a "high," for this sector was too concerned with ecclesiasticism and pageantry. To Sumner, "Broad churchmanship is scholarly and intellectual, it believes in reason and conscience as the great standards of judgment by which men are to be guided."[14]

Sumner, who increasingly managed the *Living Church*, contributed a half-dozen articles: "Ecclesiastical Trials," "The General Theological Seminary," "The Evangelical Conference and the Crisis," "The Public School Question," "The Study of the Bible," and " 'An Essay Towards Unity.' " The editorials, which were Sumner's responsibility, advocated social as well as religious unity, for the church was to promote social unity by supporting benevolent enterprises to elevate the unfortunate. Sumner in his editorials admitted that secular interests had generally created modern social-service institutions like sanatoria and orphanages, but he asserted that such institutions "would be much better and more effectual if they added to their stringent, and sometimes harsh method, the grace of *Christian* charity."[15] To Sumner, as editor and later as minister, the rationale for charity was both scientific and religious; modern science buttressed traditional religious teachings that individuals served themselves best by serving the cause of human brotherhood through self-sacrifice. Charity, whether monetary or institutional, could not solve social problems; it could only alleviate their results. Nevertheless, Christians needed to engage in philanthropic works because of pressures for the church to develop as a practical social institution and because such deeds added a personal, Christian touch to an otherwise cold, graceless routine.[16]

As Sumner later turned from the ministry to teaching and from a religious toward a secular-minded view of men and society, he shifted to guarding against irresponsible or immoral giving and to emphasizing less Christian sacrifice and brotherhood.[17] Even so, his view of charity exhibited considerable consistency from beginning to end: he held that charity must somehow be rational and controlled. And, in spite of the later impact of Naturalistic and social Darwinistic influences, he continued to believe that charity should ideally be personal and not a mere mindless function of the state. Even in 1883, in *What Social Classes Owe to Each Other*, the first major announcement of his shift in allegiance from religion to Naturalism, he wrote in the concluding chapter, "Wherefore We Should Love One Another," that the unfortunate object of charity was probably to blame, but, "It is the common frailty in the midst of a common peril which gives us a kind of solidarity of interest to rescue the one for whom the chances of life have turned out badly just now. . . . This observation, however, puts aid and sympathy in the field of private and personal relations, under the regulations of reason and conscience, and gives no ground for mechanical and impersonal schemes."[18] Throughout his lifetime, Sumner contributed at least small amounts to worthy individuals and charities.

Nevertheless, although Sumner's later position included the belief that men should love one another—or they should at least help those who fell in the race of life—he tended to emphasize antagonism among men, whether they competed or cooperated. There are significant similarities, in his early thought, to both points of view and to the relative emphasis he gave to both. For example, certain of Sumner's pronouncements in sermons and in the *Living Church* have a reformist or "social gospel" ring. His editorials advocated education for the Freedmen, fair treatment for the Indians, and improved conditions for the urban poor; but his other views revealed a more conservative tone. Concerning Indians, editorials supported a "fair-minded" Christian attempt to civilize and teach them to live properly on their reservations without their continually reverting to nomadic hunting. Patience would be required because Indians could not be expected to accept such a policy with the alacrity of civilized men. Only if fair and Christian means failed and if the Indians refused to conform to the new civilized order would a " 'blood and iron' " policy be acceptable.[19]

Of slum dwellers, Sumner's editorials noted that crime and poverty were related to crowding; and he advocated development of suburbs to counteract the implosive effect of the railroads: "It is hard to inculcate moral restraints upon people who are living crowded in cellars and garrets; it is not hard to teach them to those who live in fresh air, and light, and comparative comfort." But, in addition to an environmentalist discussion of the causes of crime, the paper argued that "These are the same everywhere. Bad passions fed by bad drink, and bad music, and laziness."[20] Furthermore, many of the poor preferred "squalor and filth with idleness, to comfort and neatness with labor."[21] And, finally, while serving the poor the church "allows the gulf between itself and modern thought, and interest, to widen and deepen, until it seems as if the great need of the Church before long would be missionaries to the educated and intelligent."[22]

In a later editorial, Sumner discussed the professions that most intimately concerned him. In America, a new, building country, those who worked with their hands were valued more than those who used their heads: "The two classes which must suffer most . . . are the clergy and college instructors—the two classes of our population who most labor for 'love' and who are least able to bear the burden, perhaps also the ones whose remonstrances are least likely to reach Washington."[23] Relative to ". . . the various gospels of 'progress,' 'labor reform,' 'woman's rights,' 'free religion,' etc., etc.," Sumner announced in the *Living Church* that "we propose to take little notice."[24] Although mildly reformist, especially in its rhetoric, the *Living Church* spoke primarily, in its editor's opinion, to the interests of scholars, clergymen, and other educated and socially conservative people. Sumner's view of this elite group's potential for social welfare and its neglected position in society was consistent and enduring.

Editing a church paper and assisting at Calvary kept Sumner well occupied, but he maintained numerous other activities during his year and summer in New York. He continued the tiresome task of translating and editing *The Books of the Kings;* and he carried on a busy social life—dined weekly with the Whitneys, saw the Godkins, made new acquaintances, courted Jeannie Elliott, gave up and returned to smoking. The effects of overwork, and perhaps of assisting a man with an imperious temperament like his own, led to conflict between Sumner and the Reverend Washburn. Although neither noted the cause, the letters they exchanged in 1870 revealed Sumner's abrasive personality. One of Sumner's letters mingled self-confession and self-righteousness; he admitted to the faults of rudeness, pride, and independence; but he concluded, "I am now satisfied that I have put myself right in this matter and you may take any course you choose. I doubt if we can ever be on cordial terms again, and I have already taken steps to secure a place."[25] Washburn's response, controlled and even kind, praised his assistant for his ability, manliness, and honesty; but he indicated, "I know both myself and you well enough to know that such a temperament must cure itself by a few hard battles of experience."[26] No evidence exists that Sumner was ever cured.

## IV    *Pastor at Morristown*

Even earlier than his conflict with Washburn, Sumner had begun to seek opportunities, but some that had come unsought included positions in Hebrew at New York's General Theological Seminary and at the Philadelphia Divinity School. Upon Sumner's request, he was ordained in 1869 as an Episcopal priest; and, after considering all positions with Jeannie Elliott and his friends, he decided to accept the rectorship that Whitney had discovered in Morristown, New Jersey, at the Church of the Redeemer. To that eminently respectable parish, the Reverend William Graham Sumner, aged thirty, moved in September 1870. After years of intensive preparation in America and Europe, he was at last an Episcopal rector.

Although he was informed that the congregation was not demanding, it was not Sumner's nature to loaf. While he performed the sundry duties of a rector, he worked especially at preaching. The more than 150 sermons he prepared, mostly at Morristown, offer extensive evidence of his early religious and social attitudes. At Morristown, as earlier, Sumner reacted negatively to revivalism and Calvinism; but he emphasized the importance of keeping not only faith but a sense of sin alive. To Sumner, enduring faith was better sustained by reason than by great surges of revivalistic enthusiasm that soon dwindled and left people numb to religious truth and feeling. His controlled and reasoned sermons reveal evidence of biblical science and scholarship, but they probably were too much in the plain style for contemporary taste or at least for that of his friend Whitney. In a letter that mixed tact with the critical assurance of the student who had taken a first in declamation at Yale to Sumner's third, Whitney argued that Sumner's sermons too much neglected manner for matter. "What I want to say is, Bill, that you *can*, if you *will*, be a great pulpit orator and do lots of good; but you must begin the writing of every sermon by reflecting on the question—How shall I impress this by figures, by illustrations, by startling language on these indifferent, listless people? Don't cover so much ground in one sermon. . . . Your great tendency is to cover too much ground and to *essay*."[27]

Despite such well-meant advice, Sumner's preaching continued to reveal his study and his belief that the ministry was a teaching and prophetic office. His parishioners were to be instructed in church history, in the creeds and sacraments, in the meaning of faith and revelation; and they were to be warned about the dangers of sin and about the need to repent and seek salvation. They were also to be alerted against the dangers and shortcomings of competing faiths and antifaiths, of rationalism, materialism, individualism, skepticism, and scientism.

In theology, Sumner regarded himself as a thoroughly orthodox Episcopalian. No liberal or modernist, he rejected Unitarianism, Emersonian Transcendentalism, and Romantic religion in general.[28]

About a fictional character, he wrote to his fiancée that "the Professor talks a great deal about 'Humanity,' the 'Universe,' 'Nature,' etc., etc., and not much about God, Christ and religion. . . . You know how far I dissent from all this. It is pantheistic and naturalistic and not religious."[29] Instead of murky Pantheism, he proposed to follow reason and the moral faculty in analyzing faith; but Sumner argued also that religion, like other world views, including rationalism and materialism, had to be based on faith. Religion was not Positivistic science; and, in the modern struggle with science, the faithful would not be overawed if they recognized "the error of believing that there is on earth any infallible authority in regard to truth."[30]

Since it was nevertheless in man's nature to attach himself to some faith, "wisdom for man consists in giving faith to, adopting and living by that theory of life which on the whole best satisfies reason and conscience, produces the purest society, develops the highest and broadest ideal of humanity." Even ignoring revelation, such pragmatic testing would ensure not only the rejection of rationalism and materialism but also the choice of revealed religion as "the best and most reasonable philosophy of life."[31] But, except for purposes of argument, Sumner was not prepared to ignore revelation, to justify Christianity purely on pragmatic grounds, or to ask parishioners to live in uncertainty. Instead, he argued that men had "sufficient means" for reaching a saving faith "and knowledge of what is right in any case." Some men asserted they had an infallible source of truth: "Some find it in the Pope, some in the Church, some in the Bible, some in conscience. I answer no—not one of those things is infallible, but all taken together as means of forming convictions, they are sufficient for the practical guidance of men in this life."[32]

The preacher's duty was to teach regarding the immediate, everyday concerns of men and to urge that his flock assume the burden of practical Christianity. Ministers could be most useful as moral teachers; for, as Sumner long believed, "The vice and misery in the world are nearly all due to moral causes. The State, in its attempts to deal with them always finds itself face to face at last with some human passion or depravity, some ignorance of moral, or politico-economical, or sanitary laws, which its statutes are powerless to deal with. These must be brought home to the convictions and intelligence of men, by other institutions, the churches and schools."[33] Numerous Sumner sermons dealt extensively with practical Christianity—with charity, stewardship, self-denial, and with individual responsibility for public and private morality. During his brief ministerial career, Sumner's emphasis on practical Christianity gradually increased as he stressed ethics somewhat more and piety somewhat less.

Sumner's religious views, like his thought generally, seemed designed to approximate a moderate or conservative Golden Mean. Mildly anti-Catholic and self-consciously American, he approved formal separation of church and state, but he maintained that the church could serve society by elevating the quality of life in a democratic republic.[34] Hardly a social gospeller, Sumner argued repeatedly in *Living Church* editorials and in sermons that the church, in its concern for the poor, neglected those who were better off and better educated. As for the work of the church in foreign fields, Sumner believed that missions contributed to the "solidarity of the human race." Of the Suez Canal, the *Living Church* had stated, "Commerce and civilization will be spread by its instrumentality, and all experience shows that these are the surest, if not the only sure basis for Christian missions."[35] Commerce, civilization, and Christianity—that great trinity so revered by late-nineteenth-century clergymen—would draw all men together in brotherhood. But for this grand work, Sumner told his fiancée in 1870, he had no talent, and he never expected to feel "the call." Some men were "called" by Providence to do their Christian duty in civilized society.[36]

## V  *Providential Design and the Kingdom of God*

Sumner's emphasis on Providential design was important to his religious faith and to his subsequent intellectual development. To Sumner, Christian faith, informed by reason and conscience, revealed God's design in both human and cosmic history. As he had learned at college, "In the heavenly bodies we see the spirit of God acting." As William Paley, the English theologian, had shown, Design proved a Designer.[37] God's plan for men, as disclosed through Christ, was that all mankind be redeemed; thus Sumner preached the ideal of the "Kingdom of God" on earth. The origins of the concept were in Christian millennialism, whose early forms had tended to stress the apocalyptic vision of the Book of Revelations concerning Christ's second coming. But, as Sumner's sermons illustrated, in respectable nineteenth-century American religious circles millennialism had been considerably domesticated: "It comes without noise or tumult, it springs in the heart of a man, in the midst of a society, and is visible only in its fruits. Wherever living fruitful faith is, wherever a sense of duty holds sway, wherever the cross of faith and duty is eagerly seized and faithfully carried, wherever sin is hated, and ignorance is banished, there is the kingdom of God."[38]

While men could promote that Utopian ideal, its ultimate fulfillment depended on God's redemptive plan; for, although proud men sought their own ends, they were only God's instruments: "Do you suppose that men who have to bear a prominent part in such movements [as the Reformation] . . . ever fully understand what they are doing? Hardly ever. Man proposes—God disposes."[39] Sumner's concept of human progress, although later much modified, originated in the determinism of supernatural design. Sumner applied his faith in design not only to his sermons but to himself, for he often marveled at his own life's course: "I never set out to 'rise in the world.' . . . I have gone on in the way that Providence opened before me step by step and have simply thought of doing my duty. . . . When I look back upon it, however, it seems almost like a romance."[40]

Sumner believed that men marched only haltingly up the path of progress because of human disabilities and because Providence used the world to test and "discipline" men. Progress entailed continual struggle, delays, disappointments, and reversals for men; but mankind's knowledge of the design that foreshadowed and directed history gave believers certainty as to its end. Although Sumner stressed human frailty and sinfulness, he also held that "it is familiar to human experience that men are capable of unlimited improvement. The divine germ may lie buried so deeply under the soil of earth that it threatens to perish there but care and nurture can make it spring and grow and bear fruit."[41] The dialectical process of struggle led inevitably toward the ultimate harmony of the Kingdom of God on earth.[42] Sumner's later Naturalistic concept of harmony as achieved through struggle derived at least partially from his religious faith in the dynamics of Providential design.

Armed with assurance of ultimate even if far-removed perfectibility, Sumner believed men could fight to establish a latter-day vision of the millennium, the Kingdom of God in America. In that struggle Providence required men to overcome the temptations of both adversity and prosperity. Thus war and peace, despair and elation, work and ease, all had disciplinary uses. But, especially, for Sumner, work, properly understood, was worship. In conceiving that men could choose to develop Providential design by building God's Kingdom, Sumner reconciled determinism and free will: men were to implement God's grand design, for they were crucially responsible for their own well being. Sumner told his fiancée, "As for trust in God, my love . . . if you were to sit down and trust in God for your dinner you would not probably get it and you would do a very wicked thing. We ought to adopt the means He has put in our power to work for what we need."[43] In a life of struggle to avoid sin and to achieve the Christian commonwealth, man's devotion to duty and his disciplined, honest work in a particular calling were divinely sanctioned; but his sloth, extravagance, intemperance, and casual trust that all would be well would be severely punished.

## VI  *Materialism and a Religious Work Ethic*

The work ethic to which Sumner applied religious sanctions was that which he had absorbed from his father and also from books and schooling. His training in the industrial virtues and in religion caused a curious ambivalence in his thinking about the life of business and pecuniary gain, but such a view was by no means unique to him as the thinking of New England Puritans centuries earlier indicates. Sumner's ambivalence derived from his concept of virtue and vice as applied to business; for although he believed that all the individual's activities should glorify his Creator, he certainly did not mean for wealthy parishioners to eschew business activity. Business, like other endeavors, served to discipline and train the human race. "True" ambition could be "noble," and business could be honorable if the individual avoided a self-congratulatory materialism by humbly recognizing the Author of his successes and if he used material gain to pursue "higher" values.

In 1872, while Sumner was summarizing and evaluating his ministry in a "Farewell Address" to his Morristown congregation before returning to Yale, he felt called to refer, as he often had, to the problem of modern materialism: "I do not deny that money has value. . . . We well know that it sets in motion all our industry and commerce and that it serves to bind human society together. . . . Money ought to be worth more to men than idleness, or discomfort, or squalor, or any physical misery, but it ought not to be worth more than honor, or affection, or patriotism, or a good conscience, or any form of duty. . . . Both in public and private trusts we want better men."[44]

Sumner's conviction about the need for better men was enduring, as the civil-service-reform views that he held throughout his career indicated. The conviction that business required better men also remained to haunt him as he moved from a religious to a Naturalistic sense of the absolute necessity for material, economic development. Early in his stay at Yale he wrote,

If I were doing no more than to teach young men how to get rich, I should think that I was not engaged in very useful business; but . . . material wealth is a necessary means to everything beyond. Many people never get beyond, either because they have all they can do to earn a living, or because they stick fast in the gilded mud. . . . If a man goes the right way to work to create wealth, it is as ennobling as any missionary work. If he goes the wrong way about it, it degrades him as much as to be a pickpocket.[45]

As a late-nineteenth-century minister, Sumner felt compelled not only to rebut any challenge that materialism, practical or philosophical, offered to religious faith, but also to maintain a delicate balance in trying to accommodate the unquestionably attractive material opportunities of the era. As the preceding discussion indicates and as Sumner's sermon on "Materialism" made clear, his method was to assert that all world views rested on faith; that a purely materialistic faith led to baseness, weakness, and despair; and that religion strengthened men to do their earthly duty in preparation for eternal life. Sumner's emphasis on the pragmatic value of religion in enlivening men to work and hope was essential to his work ethic. Although his religion faded, the moral fervor with which he exhorted men to work did not. Similarly, even though his later Naturalism brought about his stronger appreciation of wealth, his attitude to the idle rich and his rejection of money and success as ultimate ends remained constant. There always lingered in Sumner's attitude toward business a faint moralistic trace of the Puritan belief that man should use the world as if he used it not.

Sumner's enduring struggle to reconcile moral and material interests was clearly foreshadowed, as was his later Naturalism, when he asserted in a sermon of 1870 that "The first instinct of life is that of self-preservation. . . . Man has the same instinct in common with other animals"; but man's instinct of self-preservation was capable of infinite expansion. As men rose above barbarism, new desires continually appeared until a sybaritic life was sought: "Thus we see that the pursuits which absorb the attention of mankind are only developments of the primary instinct of self-preservation; we see also in how far the struggle for these things is necessary and right, and we see why it is that there is always something low and base about these merely material pursuits." [46]

Not only was man's instinct in conflict with religion, but it was apparently valid up to a point. Sumner's religiously oriented work ethic and his sense of Providential design offer clues to the origins of his Naturalism. In Sumner's thinking, God's mighty plan was gradually transmuted into nature's inexorable laws, and the ethic of the daily struggle to realize the Kingdom of God on earth tended to be transformed into one of survival value in the struggle for existence.

## VII    *Science and Religion*

In his Farewell Address to his Morristown congregation, Sumner discussed modern science which seemed as threatening to the faith as materialism. As with material pursuits, Sumner's attitudes toward scientific interests were ambiguous. During his apprenticeship and ministerial years, when considering relationships between religion and science, Sumner insisted that they belonged to different spheres and performed different, though complementary, functions. He defined "religion" in a peculiarly narrow way as synonymous with "personal religion" or "faith." Conversely, he equated "science" with "reason" or "rationalism"; and he defined it broadly as "a trained method of using the human reason." [47]

As a biblical scholar and as a "broad-church" Episcopalian, Sumner desired to "reconcile Church traditions of truth with those modern scientific and philosophical notions of truth which now so largely control the minds of men." [48] By distinguishing between faith and reason, he separated not only religion and science but also faith and theology since the latter followed rigorous methods of modern inductive science: "The principles which are so praiseworthy and so useful in science are applied directly to religion as if they must apply there equally well. . . . We need to remember that theology is one thing and personal religion is quite another. . . . Religion . . . is a matter of faith and not of reason—it is an experience of the heart and not a science nor an acquirement of the intellect." [49]

With faith placed in a protected preserve, Sumner was free to pursue science. In the "Introductory Essay" to his translation of Bähr's *Books of the Kings*, Sumner argued, "The same person approaches the Scriptures in a different frame of mind as a humble believer, and as a biblical scholar. . . . The critical scholar adopts a method of study of the Bible which would be out of place for the mass of the faithful. His negative position is only preliminary to a positive movement with efficient preparation and effective means."[50]

Critical science was barren in itself; but, if it was used in the proper religious spirit, it could reveal God's creation to man, instruct him in its laws and forces, and teach him how best to use its riches, God's gifts to men. Religious men could legitimately reject "scientific dogmatism," but not proper scientific method, for they had to face inescapable questions about "the origin of man, the age of the globe, and the unity of the races."[51] Biblical science had developed from "vulgar rationalism" to the present "critical school" which, in seeking truth, "has adopted the scientific method as the only one which can attain this object, and, as its object is to reach . . . the true biblical doctrine, it discards philosophical premises, and refuses to take laws from philosophy."[52]

The ambiguity in Sumner's sense of the relationship between science and religion was not eliminated by his attempt to keep reason and faith in separate compartments. Although Sumner's ambiguity may have been partly due to the speed with which scientific, technological influences threatened the traditional late-nineteenth-century religious world view, his personal ambivalence about the attractions of religion and of science was also reflected. Although Sumner's boyhood religion had been conventionally orthodox and at least formally evangelical, his German training had definitely converted him to biblical science, whose outlook he was clearly prepared to embrace. Thenceforward, his position, as apprentice and pastor, required him to reconcile the claims of both religion and science. Thus he insisted that the two belonged in separate but equal spheres, that from the immediate struggle would come an "ultimate reconciliation of the apparent antagonism" between the two, but that presently science threatened to establish "a dangerous dominion over the human mind."[53] As always, Sumner sought the Golden Mean in pursuance of ultimate harmony.

Consequently, in his farewell,[54] he recapitulated his views about modern religion by underlining the dangers that beset it, particularly from materialism and science, both of which encouraged skepticism. The core threat to religion—indeed, the threat of chaos for men—was that the doctrine of revelation might be overturned. As a result of this threat, churchmen had to prepare for an extended, intense battle; for "it is certain that every tradition and every inherited faith of mankind is to be staked on a reexamination of

authority and evidence within the next fifty years." In a conflict
upon which both the church and humankind depended, leaders
could not merely more sharply define and rigorously enforce dogma,
for, in combating modern philosophy and science, mere dogma was
like ancient armor against modern firearms. Instead of dogma,
ministers had to be armed, therefore, with knowledge not only of
doctrine but also of the tendencies and tools of modern philosophy
and science. Sumner concluded by asserting that it was "a childish
dream" to believe that, in the modern world, "a dogmatic Protes-
tantism can hold its creeds intact and its traditional definitions
unimpaired"; but he reiterated his faith in biblical revelation and
denied that "the great doctrines of God, immortality, redemption,
forgiveness of sins, and divine Providence are to disappear in a
conflict from which philosophic rationalism, or naturalistic materialism shall emerge sole and sovereign over the faith of men."

When Sumner prepared in 1872 to enter the academic battlefield
as a challenger against the aggressive claims of modern philosophy
and science, he was eager to use their methods and insights where
appropriate, but he was committed to preserve religious fundamen-
tals. Nevertheless, his long-term pattern of intellectual development
was to be from religion to "science" and Naturalism—an evolution
that had begun during his German stay, if not during his college
days. In fact, it is ironical that Sumner, early to enlist for the battle
against science, was almost immediately captured. But, then, he had
been at least half-a-hostage for several years.

## VIII    Farewell to the Ministry

In his farewell address, Sumner also discussed the ministry by
recalling his feelings upon arriving at Morristown—his sense of
inexperience and his "academical and literary" preferences. But he
had also come with definite beliefs and aims: he had firmly believed
that the church had to be a living institution and that the minister,
like the Hebrew prophets, had to speak as "a free, original, bold,
and energetic instructor if he is to be a power in our modern
society." Sumner could not be a clergyman "with an amateur or
dilettante knowledge of music, architecture, and decoration, or a
gentleman of elegant leisure petted and admired within a certain
wealthy circle, which he and his handsome church serve to orna-
ment"; an ecclesiastical functionary; or "mouthpiece of tradition."
Since "God has given me no gifts to fit me for any such position,"
Sumner avowed that he had to "strive by study, reflection, and

thought to vindicate and enforce the facts and laws which constitute truth upon the minds and consciences of men."

But the American minister, Sumner asserted, was forced to dissipate his energies. As preacher, he was expected to play the scholar; as pastor, the genial caller and host. Required to be all things to all parishioners, the minister's preaching almost inevitably descended to the "commonplace and drivel." Sumner, who dreaded and had fought against such a descent, believed that "the duty of preaching, that is of persuading men's minds and informing their consciences by acute thought and living speech is secondary to no duty of the Christian minister."

Sumner's farewell address emphasized two of the three major aspects of his personality. It illustrated, first, his attraction to the elitist and prophetic role of the moral teacher. In an early sermon of 1869 he had declared that "to direct the current, to lead the popular opinion, to teach the community and to govern its movements, is the prerogative of the highest genius. Those who are called of God to do this are prophets and apostles."[55] Preaching, he told Jeannie Elliott, gave him "a great power" and "such influence that I find I can get these people to do what I want them to do in many things."[56]

Second, Sumner's farewell address underlined his preference for scholarship and the study. In his earlier days, religion had served various purposes. It had offered emotional release to a youth who was at least repressed, if not deprived, emotionally. His early sermons, which appealed to the affective nature, expressed that release in formal terms. His European journal reference to Hattie Morgan, to his mother, and to his assurance that Providence directed his destiny indicated that religion continued for a time to offer him emotional solace. Third, religion also offered young Sumner release from a low social class position and the higher status that his father at least implicitly had encouraged him to seek and that Dr. Beadle had embodied. Religion offered piety, respectability, a scholarly life—for all of which Sumner yearned; but, in time, religion became for Sumner more a subject of study and less a matter of worship.

In 1872, aged thirty-two, Sumner left the ministry expecting never to return. The moment was propitious. For, in the post-Civil War era, the pulpit was giving way to the lectern as a major forum for discussion of public questions. In turning to the academy, Sumner turned as well from biblical scholarship to political econ-

omy, political science, history, and sociology—and he did so when
secular scholarship was increasingly prestigious. Finally, and not
incidentally, within a few years following 1872 Sumner had clearly
moved from a religious world view to Scientism and Naturalism.

As a young man Sumner believed that his life pattern, which led
from anonymity toward success, had been directed by Providence:
he had been "called." One can accept the sincerity of his belief that
Providential design extended even to himself, and one can also
notice that his faith had pragmatic consequences. Although always
apparently self-confident, Sumner found in design assurance of his
destiny as a useful and successful servant of God. Design also
ensured that he was not solely responsible for his actions and
decisions. When entering the ministry, he was aware that status and
respectability were attractive, but he had been "called." When he
was "called" from Morristown to Yale, he was clearly aware of his
own potentialities and preferences, for he had studied them. There
is no need to argue that, in accepting his call to Yale, Sumner also
seized upon the main chance, for his inner life was considerably too
complex to depend on conscious hypocrisy for its actions. But it
would be misleading to suggest that he was merely fortunate in
discovering that his "call" to Yale and his personal preference were
entirely synonymous.

It would be equally misleading to intimate that in 1872, or at any
time, Sumner's character and motivations were entirely understandable to an observer. His own limited testimony, and that of others,
reveals an intensely private and introverted personality. Publicly he
became, especially in his later years as a scientific sociologist, a
rigorous critic of religion, not only of its institutional aspects but
also of its central tendency to mask reality with superstition.
Privately, Sumner's religious attitudes may have been less antagonistic and more traditional than his public statements. Although he
left the ministry in 1872, he never left the Episcopal priesthood, for
he was reported annually as detailed to Yale. He once returned to
his robes to baptize a grandson; a Yale student was once shocked to
discover Professor Sumner taking up collection at New Haven's
Trinity Episcopal Church; and Sumner reportedly took communion
not long before his last illness.[57] Such evidence is ambiguous, for it
may merely indicate Sumner's willingness to follow certain expected
forms. "I never consciously gave up a religious belief," Sumner
once said. "It was as if I had put my beliefs into a drawer, and when
I opened it there was nothing there at all."[58]

CHAPTER 3

# Yale and the Wider World

WHEN Sumner had been offered a tutorship at Yale in 1866, he had felt the comedown from Göttingen and Oxford; but, although he was unwilling four years later to be a tutor again, he had nevertheless asserted that he loved old Yale and wanted to return to it as a professor.[1] In the summer of 1870, when he had accepted the Morristown position, he and his fiancée had anxiously sought his true calling; and Jeannie had concluded that he had two callings, either in a pastorate or a professorship, because "in either one you will have time to read and study which you like to do and at the same time you will feel that you are helping along your fellow-men."[2] Although teaching positions and salaries were limited, Sumner and Jeannie had agreed that a professorship at $3,000 was preferable to preaching for $5,000, especially since there would be other kinds of compensations.[3] Sumner had believed that in a college town like Cambridge, Massachusetts, or New Haven, Connecticut, faculty families *were* society; and he had written that their " 'position' is certainly very good, much better I think than a clergyman's."[4] Moreover, Jeannie, whom he was to marry in 1871, had wanted to escape New York City's "show and extravagance" and "be in the society of cultivated people" who had "aims above making money and spending it to make a display."[5] Her inquiries had revealed that a professor's wife needed only "one good black silk dress" for the balls and that a college town "seems to be the only place where poverty is respectable."[6]

Consequently, Sumner had tried to raise funds to endow a chair or new professorship at Yale.[7] In talks with his friends, he had focused on his financial and his political problems because Yale had limited resources and because he had antagonized various faculty members as an outspoken tutor. He had, however, also made friends among the faculty and the alumni, particularly among the younger alumni. In those days, Yale's half-dozen tutors taught half the courses, and Sumner had excelled among tutors and even faculty, some of whom he had described condescendingly as a "Puritan theological crowd."[8] In 1872, when Sumner was asked to teach either Greek or political and social science at Yale, he wrote to Yale's president, Noah Porter, that "I can only say that I greatly prefer the chair of political science. If they put me in it I will make it my life work. That chair at Yale could be made most influential on the future of this country."[9] In later years, Sumner was sometimes disturbed by conditions at Yale and by his position in life, but he never regretted leaving the pulpit. While overworking at the college and testifying in Washington about a currency bill in the early 1870s, he wrote that Yale brought him "into contact with active public life, which I enjoy, and . . . is connected with most important public interests. I am very glad that I was able to escape from parish life, and from theology altogether."[10]

## I   Educational Reform

A weak Yale faculty, barren classrooms, and a library nearly as barren had made Sumner a radical educational reformer before he returned to the college in 1872. Influenced like other forward-looking scholars by the German model, he had become a leader in the late 1860s of the "Young Yale" movement to modernize the old institution and especially to have alumni named to the governing College Corporation in order to counterbalance a set of self-perpe-tuating Congregational ministers. The "Young Yale" group had hoped that antiquated theological traditions could thereby be altered, that seasoned scholars could replace green tutors, and that more courses in the physical and social sciences and in modern languages could be introduced. "Young Yale" had won a victory in 1871 when Connecticut's legislature had replaced state senators with Yale alumni on the College Corporation.[11]

Sumner's major contribution to the controversy had been to insist that modernization required money. In the *Nation* of September 8, 1870, he had discussed the "mercantile problem" of procuring funds to hire superior scholars as merely a case of supply and demand, for "Professors or potatoes, the law is universal." Sumner had asserted that Yale needed businesslike fund-raising from two major sources—from many small contributors who could revive the college while potential large contributors dallied and from students who should expect to pay higher tuition for high quality education.[12] Moreover, Sumner believed that it was as crucial to sever old ecclesiastical ties as to develop new financial ties, for he had commented in an 1870 *Living Church* editorial that secularized education would prevail over all opposition. Although he had admitted that parents opposed eliminating religious training, he had argued that recent college graduates felt differently; but he had also asserted that modern society needed universities because they were "properly conservative forces," that they should be created from existing colleges, and that "it will be very fortunate if the old institutions, which have history and reputation and traditions, can lead the way."[13]

The fundamental reform for the "Young Yale" movement was to modernize curriculum, a task to which Sumner dedicated a working lifetime. To Sumner, modernity required that the rigid program of his student days give way to greater student choice, but he also opposed uncontrolled student electives among courses. As an educational "radical," Sumner always argued that, to prepare graduates for contemporary life, Yale needed a broader curriculum in the physical and social sciences, greater allowance for specialization, and lessened emphasis on the Classics. Partly because of Sumner's long-term influence and faculty committee work, Yale's curriculum was gradually reformed; and Yale gradually followed the modern trend among American universities—despite continuing opposition from important faculty and administrators which included the classicist President Porter. Until Sumner retired, he stressed that "those men who think that the classics will recover their ascendancy in education are like bats in sunshine. . . . Greek is dead and philosophy is moribund. If we stick to them they will sink us."[14]

## II  *Value of Education*

When Sumner thought of his purpose as an educator at Yale, opportunity was his touchstone. Few men could have been more intensely aware than he was of the opportunities that education offered or of the dramatic changes in prospects and social position that followed from a good education. Although Sumner generally advocated laissez-faire policies, he had no qualms about the need to support public schools financially, at least with local and state funds. His reasons, which he had first stated fully in his 1870 *Living Church* editorial "The Public School Question," were consistent through a long career: public schooling offered protection to a democratic republic and opportunity for individual self-realization. The issue was not merely whether there would be Catholic parochial schools or Bible reading but whether "the American social and political system" would endure. To reverse the historical trend from sectarian to public education would create "a terrible menace to our social and political system, which is yet an experiment, the success of which depends on the development and perfection of the common school system."[15]

In the 1870 article, Sumner had supported his position by comparing parochial and public education and by asking, "Shall we teach children to do certain things because the teacher commands them, and not to do others because they are forbidden; or shall we teach them to think and see for themselves? . . . Shall we teach them intelligent judgment, or implicit obedience to authority?" Should teachers, Sumner had continued, determine what students should know, or should teachers lead their charges into the "boundless field" of human knowledge and potential? Minds taught to ask "why" could never be "compressed into a traditional system."[16] During Sumner's more than twenty-five years on the Connecticut State Board of Education, he continued to favor compulsory public education because "incapacity to think" was "a social crime."[17] Although Sumner generally rejected the theory that men had natural rights, he virtually made an exception of educational opportunity, as when he responded to William C. Whitney's inquiry about women students: "My own view is that Yale College ought to be open to all mortals who want to study, black, white, red, yellow, male, female, handsome, ugly, etc., etc."[18]

Sumner recognized risks in educating everyone, because "at the same time that it differentiates the leaders, popular education plants the seeds of undiscipline in their subordinates" and thus made "social war" inevitable.[19] To Sumner, popular education was a radical force that generated fundamental, often unforeseen, and sometimes virtually uncontrollable social changes. Paradoxically, however, popular education promoted social stability not only because it disseminated social customs and mores widely and thus homogenized a population diverse in class and ethnic terms but also because it elevated and differentiated members of the masses and thus offset the leveling effects of democracy. On balance, Sumner believed that the risks of popular education were necessary because his view, like that of Thomas Jefferson, was that public education identified and trained leaders who initiated creative social change.[20]

Sumner knew, however, that the results of popular education were varied and unpredictable and that the same was true of education generically. Although education offered individuals no guarantee of a successful life, it gave them the opportunity to prepare to take advantage of the chances of existence in a life that was essentially determined for most men. Moreover, education provided individuals and society with no assurance of physical, moral, or social progress because knowledge was a power that could be used for good or evil. To Sumner, the faith that men would inevitably use knowledge for good was a superstition of his era.[21]

Nevertheless, the alternative to popular education—widespread ignorance and indoctrination of the masses—was intolerable to Sumner. It was thus his duty to cleanse education of superstition by clarifying its purpose, which was to offer the individual useful knowledge and to discipline him so that he would think clearly and independently. Since education would develop enlightened views, mankind, freed from illusions, would come to know reality. As Sumner came in the 1870s to be influenced by a social Darwinian conception of reality that stressed conflict, he increasingly viewed education as a tool that enabled men to adapt to environment and thereby to survive or to advance in the struggle for existence, but he did not change his ideal of the men that education should produce. Such disciplined and courageous leaders could resist Romantic illusions about man's lot, irrational crowd pressures, and popularity's siren song; they could advance the public interest; and they could thereby contribute to Sumner's social ideal of harmonious integration.[22] Yet, as a competitive scholar and as a social Darwinist, Sumner believed that harmonious integration developed from conflict because he was convinced that the dynamics of learning depended on the clash of opposing viewpoints. His contemporary Justice Oliver Wendell Holmes used an image that was entirely compatible with Sumner's understanding when he observed that society benefited from competition in the marketplace of ideas.

### III    *Teacher*

Over many years hundreds of Yale students, who regarded Sumner as an awesome character and as an authoritative scholar, usually voted him, especially early in his career, as one of their more popular teachers; and they often applauded and cheered him at the end of a course. As a disciplinarian with a dozen rules and as a commanding personality and character, he lectured not only as an academician but as a public man who knew statesmen and financiers, who engaged in public controversies, and who testified on the currency and taxation before Congress. Although he was reserved and often did not know students by name, he stirred and prodded and required them to learn. As a Yale graduate remembered, "he was a prodigious personality, something cold and massive and autocratic. He came stalking into the classroom with a sort of 'Be damned to you' air."[23] President William Howard Taft recalled that Sumner "had more to do with stimulating my mental activities than anyone under whom I studied during my entire course."[24] Sumner was helpful to graduate students, to the extent requested; and with them he was less dogmatic and more willing to reveal his doubts than with undergraduates.

Alumni spoke with respect and affection of "Billy" Sumner, and they invariably spoke of his masculinity because he had become a cult figure at Yale, living proof that a gentleman and scholar could also be manly. In later years, students nicknamed the pioneer sociologist "Old Mores"; but still they applauded him because he taught them about the mysteries and harsh necessities of a Naturalistic world they would soon enter. Sumner poured great energies into teaching because of his sense of duty, but he undoubtedly also did so because he found gratifying the opportunity to instruct and the adulation it provided.[25]

Although Sumner sought unremittingly to realize his educational ideal of teaching students to integrate harmoniously with society and yet to retain their individuality, his students learned much from his personal example about individuality and considerably less about harmony. An outspoken and sometimes rude partisan, Sumner made strong friends and strong enemies. With faculty friends, whom he remembered as few, he exchanged professional information and commiserated about overwork and ill health, but toward those who opposed educational reform he was provocative and sometimes sarcastic. Even of a departmental colleague, he said privately that "every idea comes to him in a fog, *and—whirling*."[26]

## IV   *Nineteenth-Century Liberal*

Sumner made his reputation not only as an aggressive teacher and educational reformer within Yale but as an equally aggressive lecturer and writer about public issues. In both realms, Sumner was dedicated to advancing human welfare which, as he could testify personally, was very much a matter of hard work. Those conversant with his work have found its intensity and extensiveness remarkable, for he worked eight to twelve hours daily, wore out, and yet carried on. Even as early as 1874 Sumner wrote to Lord Campbell that "I

have been very busy, and am all fagged out. I must struggle on a
month more before vacation, but I sometimes fear I may break
down entirely. I do not dare to let my wife know how ill and tired I
am."[27]

Work dedicated to the interest of human welfare also depended
upon efficient organization, and Sumner paid considerable attention
to it, particularly when he collected sociological data. His successor
in sociology at Yale, Albert Galloway Keller, estimated that for the
projected "Science of Society" Sumner collected and filed—without
graduate student assistants—more than 150,000 notes from sources
in the dozen languages that he read. His cross-referenced note
system filled fifty-two file cabinet drawers; and he used varied
symbols for headings, different colored note papers, and rubber-
faced type for bibliographic references.[28]

The product of such organized and hard-driven intelligence was
a mass of publications and manuscripts; Sumner published from
1872 to 1906 a dozen books. His writings typically addressed matters
of political economy and political science—the currency and banking, protectionism and free trade, politics in a democracy, civil-
service reform, and arguments for laissez-faire policies. At least half
of his books addressed issues of his day. Of *A History of American
Currency*, he remarked that "it was written in great haste in the
spring of 1874 to catch up with Congress which was discussing
inflation."[29] Although Sumner's works were not vague polemics but
were based on research, none of his issue-oriented books outlived its
author in usefulness or in influence.

In his books and essays, Sumner spoke as a nineteenth-century
liberal or "Mugwump," a Republican who bolted for Democrat
Grover Cleveland when James G. Blaine gained the Republican
nomination for President in 1884. More broadly, the Mugwump
liberal was generally a conservative, educated Protestant with
upper-middle-class ideals who saw himself as one of the elite.
Whether wealthy or not, the Mugwump disliked and feared plutocracy, the laboring lower classes, and social polarization. Motivated
by moral concern and perhaps by fears of social displacement,
Mugwump liberals sought to restore former conditions by supporting "sound" classical economics, laissez-faire competition, lower
tariffs, and the gold standard. Politically, liberals advocated an
honest and an efficient government by the best men through
supporting civil-service reform and through attacking machine
politics and corruption.

About the abilities of the masses—notably the blacks and the urban immigrants—the liberals were uncertain; and they wavered between commitment to and disdain for democracy. Indeed, nineteenth-century liberals tended to believe that an infusion of honesty could reform even democratic government, could bring under control not only the demos but also a threatening plutocracy of monopolistic corporations—and could thus establish a degree of social harmony. Nevertheless, they believed that Utopia was unlikely to emerge even if the government were reformed, for many social evils that resulted from the struggle for existence and lower-class improvidence were irremediable.[30] These views virtually characterize Sumner's social, economic, and political ideas as he expressed them in his publications.

As a nineteenth-century liberal, Sumner approached his work of reforming social evils through publicizing economic and political truths with high seriousness, deep moral indignation, and a jabbing pen. In 1885 his Preface to *Protectionism: The -Ism Which Teaches That Waste Makes Wealth* noted that he had directly involved himself in the era's three great issues—the currency, civil-service reform, and protectionism—and that he had addressed the present book to intelligent voters without bothering "to keep or to throw off scientific or professional dignity." "Protectionism," Sumner wrote, "seems to me to deserve only contempt and scorn, satire and ridicule. . . . Still . . . I have . . . undertaken a patient and serious exposition of it."[31]

Despite his stated sober intent, however, Sumner's references to "protectionists of stupid good faith," to "protectionists for hire and those by election," and to "protectionists who run colleges, and those who want to burn colleges down" revealed the moralistic rather than the scientific dynamic behind the book's purpose. "Protectionism arouses my moral indignation," Sumner wrote, "which . . . draws me away from the scientific pursuits which form my real occupation, and forces me to take part in a popular agitation. The doctrine of a 'call' applies in such a case."[32] As earlier and as always, Sumner had been "called" to a task of sacrifice and service that would benefit society.

Despite Sumner's research and his social-scientific intent, moralism permeated his books. In *Andrew Jackson as a Public Man: What He Was, What Chances He Had, and What He Did with Them* (1882)—perhaps the best researched of his biographies and certainly the best written—he examined political and Constitutional issues, economic development, and domestic and diplomatic matters relating to foreign trade. His overarching interpretation was similar to the "patrician school" of nineteenth-century historians in that it described the victorious—though to Sumner unfortunate—struggle of democracy against the bonds of Constitutionalism. A concluding passage exhibits the strength of Sumner's ironical style as well as his distaste for Jackson: "He had had honors beyond anything which his own heart had ever coveted. His successes had outrun his ambition. . . . He had been idolized by the great majority. . . . He had been thwarted in hardly anything. . . . In his last years he joined the church, and . . . professed to forgive all his enemies in a body. It does not appear that he ever repented of anything, ever thought that he had been in the wrong in anything, or ever forgave an enemy as a specific individual."[33]

In *Alexander Hamilton* (1890) Sumner analyzed his subject's influence on the new nation. His background chapters stressed the "defects and faults" of American public life from 1765 to 1780 which included "social discord and mobs," the persecution of Tories, "spurious patriotism," the currency, the "tyranny of Committees," factions, military undiscipline, and "social disintegration." To Sumner, Hamilton had been "one of the leading heroes" in the great work of sufficiently centralizing the new nation's power to forestall movements to repudiate public and private debts and to overcome anarchistic elements. Nevertheless, Sumner believed that Hamilton had ruined himself in a rising democracy by attempting with his imperious and aristocratic air to force reforms. Sumner judged that Hamilton's economic and financial contributions "have been greatly exaggerated."[34] Only a year later Sumner published *The Financier and the Finances of the American Revolution*, and in 1892 an abridgment which focused on Robert Morris,[35] but all three works, which were written when Sumner was under severe mental and physical strain, are uninspiring.

*What Social Classes Owe to Each Other*, which appeared in 1883, was one of two Sumner books that were later reprinted. This well-written series of essays, which documents his transition from religion to Naturalism, is an argument for laissez-faire which denies that " 'the State' owes anything to anybody except peace, order, and the guarantees of rights."[36] As always, Sumner denied that the "rich, comfortable, prosperous, virtuous, respectable, educated, and healthy" owed anything except as humane and charitable men to the "less fortunate or less successful in the struggle for existence."[37]

*What Social Classes Owe to Each Other* early established and
helped to maintain Sumner's reputation as a social Darwinist.

The moral concern evident in Sumner's books was fundamental
to his thought, and it was especially evident in his essays, which
were intended for intelligent but not necessarily highly educated
citizens. Although Sumner habitually used a logical and argumentative organization, he followed his college training and believed
that "book learning is addressed to the intellect, not to the feelings,
but the feelings are the spring of action."[38] It was second nature for
Sumner to appeal to the reader's moral faculty when he discussed
public questions. His essays were clearly expressed and often biting,
but they were not polished stylistically because of his manifold
responsibilities and his numerous publications. In addition to his
books, he published perhaps two hundred essays and speeches.

As his views developed and matured from 1876 to 1886, approximately forty-eight articles appeared; but from 1887 through 1890
he published about sixty more. Over forty of these were in a series
for the *Independent,* but he also wrote for *Popular Science Monthly,
Forum, Chautauquan, Rand McNally's Banker's Monthly, Cosmopolitan, Nation, Twentieth Century,* and *Frank Leslie's Illustrated
Newspaper.* Given his other work in the late 1880s—which included
the preparation of two or three books—it is not surprising that
Sumner's health broke down. From 1891 to 1896 he published only
four articles and two books; in 1896 he published a dozen articles
and a book; but thereafter, partly because of ill health but primarily
because of his gradual shift from political economy and political
science to sociological research, he was no longer one of America's
more prolific polemicists. From 1897 to 1909 he published only
about twenty articles which was still almost two a year but far fewer
than when he was at his peak.

Like his books, most of Sumner's articles focused on such political
and economic matters as reforming politics in democracy by eliminating corruption through civil-service examinations, by reforming
the currency in accord with the gold standard, by excising the
cancer of protectionism so that free trade could flourish, and by
defending freedom in the industrialization process. In his essays and
in his speeches, as in his teaching, he defended the doctrines of
classical economics and republican government by discussing contemporary issues—which undoubtedly increased the attention he
commanded at Yale and in the press. Fewer than a dozen articles
bearing directly on sociology appeared, and four of these were
published in 1909.

## V  *Controversial Polemicist*

Sumner always seemed impelled to speak his mind open
even harshly, no doubt because he was driven by concern tha
prevail; but he just as certainly personalized the issues. His vigorous
and sometimes brutal essays, which tended to question the intelligence, sincerity, or masculinity of his opponents, seemed designed
to elicit replies in kind so that constant attacks beat upon Sumner in
the press and in his mail. Some reactions were reasoned criticisms of
his more extreme laissez-faire and social Darwinist positions, but
other reactions were intemperate and eccentric. A typical letter
suggested that, in *What Social Classes Owe to Each Other*, Sumner
had exhibited "the flunkyism which follows the shadow of wealth."[39]
Apparently hoping that readers would take Sumner less seriously,
his adversaries sometimes rose above mere ill temper to satire and
doggerel:

The Political Economist and the Tramp
(Dedicated to Prof. W. G. Sumner, of Yale.)
by Phillips Thompson

Walking along a country road,
　While yet the morning air was damp,
As unreflecting, on I strode,
　I marked approach the frequent tramp.

The haggard, ragged, careworn man
　Accosted me in plaintive tone,
"I must have food—" he straight began;
　"Vile miscreant," I cried, "begone!

" 'Tis contrary to every rule
　That I my fellows should assist;
I'm of the scientific school,
　Political-economist.

"Dost thou not know, deluded one,
　That Adam Smith has clearly proved
That 'tis self-interest alone
　By which the wheels of life are moved?

"That competition is the law
　By which we either live or die;
I've no demand thy labor for,
　Why, then, should I thy wants supply?

"And Herbert Spencer's active brain
   Shows how the social struggle ends;
The weak die out, the strong remain;
   'Tis this that Nature's plan intends.

"Now really 'tis absurd of you
   To think I'd interfere at all;
Just grasp the scientific view,
   The weakest must go to the wall."

My words impressed his dormant thought;
   "How wise," he said, "is Nature's plan;
Henceforth I'll practice what you've taught
   And be a scientific man.

"We are alone—no others near
   Or even within hailing distance;
I've a good club, and now right here
   We'll have a struggle for existence.

"The weak must die—the strong survive.
   Let's see who'll prove the harder hittist,
So if you wish to keep alive
   Prepare to prove yourself the fittest.

"If you decline the test to make
   And doubt your chances of survival,
Your watch and pocket-book I'll take,
   As competition strips a rival."

What could I do but yield the point,
   Though conscious of no logic blunder;
And as I quaked in every joint,
   The tramp departed with his plunder.[40]

Displeasure at Sumner's public pronouncements was sometimes less innocuous and amusing, for his attack on the Spanish-American War brought calls for his dismissal from Yale. The free-trade stand of this "flunky of wealth" irritated many wealthy interests and led a faculty member in one case to suggest to a complainant against Sumner that it would be "indelicate" of the Yale College Corporation to silence Professor Sumner "unless he teaches something immoral or unchristian."[41] Unfortunately for Sumner, many protectionists defined free-trade in exactly those terms. Consequently,

Sumner had to be careful when, for example, he felt impelled to decline an invitation to a free-trade dinner that would cause him to miss classes: "If I cut for any free-trade occasion I should give a chance to the adversary."[42]

## VI  *Politics*

Always concerned about influencing public policy, Sumner participated directly in New Haven politics for a few years; but his major contribution was to write and lecture widely about public issues. In 1872, until the protectionist tariff advocate Horace Greeley was nominated, Sumner supported the Liberal Republican movement because it opposed continued Reconstruction in the South. Sumner was elected as a Republican New Haven alderman in 1873; but, despite his growing reputation at the state level, Sumner bolted the Republicans in 1876 because, as he told students, he preferred Samuel Tilden, "hard money, free trade and local self-government" to the Republican's mediocre Rutherford B. Hayes.[43] The Democrats in 1876 quickly named Sumner as one of several "visiting statesmen" who were sent to investigate charges of vote frauds in Louisiana's contested presidential election. Sumner's independence made him a pariah with the Republicans; and, although the Democrats nominated him for a third term as alderman, he was defeated. He did not reenter politics, and he later wrote in an "Autobiographical Sketch" of 1903 that he had not known "the rules of the game and did not want to learn them. Therefore, the adepts at it could play with me in more senses than one. My experience, however, has . . . enabled me to gauge the value of the talk we hear about 'civics' and 'citizenship.' "[44]

Sumner nevertheless maintained a lively interest in political matters. In 1880, since he opposed the major candidates and of course the Greenback party's James B. Weaver, he discarded his ballot. Unable to swallow the tainted James G. Blaine in 1884, Sumner turned as a Mugwump to Grover Cleveland, who, even if larger, was more palatable; and he supported Cleveland again in 1888 for his low tariff views.

Sumner's later voting is not recorded; but protectionist William McKinley, Populist William Jennings Bryan, and a Theodore Roosevelt who blustered against big business and extolled the strenuous imperial virtues were anathema to nineteenth-century laissez-faire liberals like Sumner. "We shall all have to vote for Teddy in 1908 in order to ward off Bryan and Hades," Sumner wrote in 1906, but "if

I do it (vote for Teddy) I shall be disgraced forever."[45] Sumner's reference to Hades may seem hyperbolic; but he believed that John Peter Altgeld, the notorious defender of the Chicago Haymarket anarchists, might be made a member of Bryan's cabinet.[46] In 1908 Sumner was probably willing to vote for his former student, William Howard Taft, in order to ward off not only Bryan and Hades but also Socialist Eugene V. Debs.

### VII   *Scholar's Travail*

Ill health, the burdens of domestic life, and perennial money worries repeatedly intruded on Sumner's work. When he broke down in 1890, he was virtually incapacitated by a "nervous illness" that was a common malady of the intellectual elite of his age.[47] In December 1890, as he prepared to sail for Europe, Sumner wrote to William C. Whitney that "the bottom fact is my brain and nerves" and that "a fortnight ashore over there" would help him "brace up so as to get through the year." Whitney had apparently urged his ill friend to accept financial help, for Sumner had admitted that "what I need, however, beyond all question, is a year of rest. If any such thing as you mentioned could be carried out I am in no position to refuse it from my friends."[48] Subsequently, Sumner had a friend prepare a list of "not all Bones men, but men of means whom he thought friends of mine";[49] and he received in 1891 a fund to help defray the cost of a teaching replacement at Yale and the expense of a year in Europe from forty-two subscribers, who included Henry Holt, Cornelius Vanderbilt, Chauncey Depew, and Whitney.[50]

Since Sumner recovered only slowly from his nervous ailment, he was forced to limit public lectures and social appearances and to publish less. Increasing debility eventually forced him to relinquish his "Science of Society" project; but, even after a stroke in 1907 had incapacitated his right arm for months, he made and dated minor corrections on manuscripts in a painfully shaky left-handed scrawl. Sumner's last illness resulted from a stroke which he suffered in New York City in December 1909, where he had gone, although ailing, to give the presidential address before the American Sociological Society.[51]

After his departure from Yale in 1909. Sumner had told Albert Galloway Keller that he actually enjoyed retirement; for he had escaped the perennial eight-thirty class and could have late break-fasts and long hours with his wife. Jeannie Sumner had been reared in easy circumstances, had married a devoted husband who was nevertheless absorbed in college and national affairs, and had become "delicate and ailing" like so many middle-class, nineteenth-century women.[52] Friends often mentioned her visits to rest sanitariums and her "invalidism." The Sumners worked to maintain an affectionate relationship, but Jeannie's recurrent illnesses imposed considerable strains on an habitually overburdened scholar. Nevertheless, Sumner tried to carry domestic burdens with good grace, for he viewed the family as a refuge from the harsh realities of academic and public conflict.

In fact, Sumner distinguished sharply between the professional realm of men and the social realm which focused primarily on his wife and sons and a few friends. Although hard and cold among men, Sumner was a loving husband, a solicitous host, and a concerned and dutiful father. In the latter capacity, he wrote a classic letter of advice to his elder son, Eliot:

You know that I have never wanted you to suffer by poverty or to go in for anything luxurious. Try to settle yourself . . . in rooms and board on the same principles and I will meet the expense. I have never felt any dissatisfaction about your demands on me for money, except in regard to one or two extra things like society expenses, etc. But I think nothing of those things now. . . . Be economical, but live as you have been brought up. . . . Write to your mama every Sunday or oftener and to me whenever you like. Let me know all the *cold* facts—how it seems, etc., etc. I should be glad if you would take me into your confidence. If I know the facts I can do a great deal probably. . . . Remember all I have said to you about seizing your chances energetically, about being enterprising, and about women."[53]

To protect and prepare his sons required money as well as love and concern; but, as Sumner had written in 1870, "teaching is really, in this country, a sort of missionary labor. One must deny one's self and make all sorts of sacrifices in order to educate men in things which enable them to earn wealth and fame. This is not right. I do not believe that it can long remain so."[54] Sumner came to regard himself as a dismal prophet. He told Albert Galloway Keller that wealthy "Bill Whitney lay back and roared, as if it were a nigger-show joke, when I told him that my salary had been raised $250 fifteen years ago."[55] The Sumners got along, but not in luxury. Sumner imagined having a yacht on which to entertain his friends, and he wished he could leave a fortune to a new grandson; but, as he had written to Eliot, a man should not seek luxury but comfort. At least partly because Sumner lectured and published widely, his family managed to keep servants, to recuperate at the shore, to travel occasionally to Europe, and to buy some American Telephone and Telegraph Company stock. Sumner was not only a polemicist and scholar from a sense of civic duty but also from a sense of duty to support his family and himself in genteel comfort. Despite Sumner's best efforts, however, none of his books made much money; and even though *Folkways* made more than any of his other books, his first annual royalty check was for only about $60. How much money his lectures and articles earned is uncertain, but $400 or $500 a year would have significantly increased his income. Yet, despite his difficulties in achieving financial comfort as a Yale professor, Sumner hardly considered another occupation or position except during the crisis over his use of a textbook by Herbert Spencer.[56]

Late in his career, Sumner told Albert Galloway Keller that "it is now 10:30. If I could afford it, my resignation would be in by noon."[57] As he neared retirement, Sumner told Keller, "I am not going to resign to suit you. I *want* to resign if I can get a pension on which I can live."[58] Sumner was undoubtedly serious in both instances; for, if he had been freed from teaching and administrative duties, he could have concentrated on his "Science of Society." Old Yale and its "boys" meant much to Sumner, for they had given him rewards as well as pain; but they were nevertheless secondary to his consuming commitment to sociological studies and to his search for understanding and harmony in a universe that, with the decline of religious faith and the rise of Naturalistic assumptions, seemed increasingly alien and hostile to man.

CHAPTER 4

# From Political Economy to Sociology

IN 1872, when Sumner had assumed his duties in the newly created chair of political and social science at Yale, one of his first tasks had been to clarify both the terms and the boundaries of this new and virtually undefined area of academic interest. From the beginning of his academic career, therefore, Sumner was a pioneer on the trail that led ultimately to modern sociology. The trail head was, of course, in territory familiar to Sumner: the discipline then known as political economy, which was roughly equivalent to modern economics. Political economy, Sumner told students in his "Introductory Lecture to Courses in Political and Social Science" of 1873, was a branch of political science that had "the most vital importance for the American people. . . . I affirm that the questions on which our national future to-day depend are questions of political economy, questions of labor and capital, of finance and taxation. . . . The duty of the economist is not simply to learn how to avoid waste of what has been won but to learn the laws by which there may be no falling short of the utmost that might be attained; and the duty of the social scientist is to teach that moral and social deterioration follows inevitably upon economical mistakes."[1]

Sumner revealed the religious underpinning of his moralistic attitude to questions of political economy in another lecture of the early 1870s which addressed the vexing problem of materialism. The young professor, only a few years removed from sermons on the same subject, emphasized that, in seeking to become a science which taught men how to gather wealth, political economy did not deny the higher aspects of life; for, as a specialized discipline, it merely showed men how to take the necessary first steps toward the higher good. Political economy sought to find and to teach men about the laws of production and distribution "which are fixed in the order of the universe. We may go farther and say God's laws."[2]

59

## I  *Classical Economics*

The economic laws of God which Sumner taught in his early and middle years at Yale were the laws of classical economics which had been discovered in the late-eighteenth and early-nineteenth centuries by Adam Smith, Thomas Robert Malthus, and David Ricardo, those English economists who, Sumner continued to assert at least as late as the late 1880s, "have given us all the political economy we possess."[3] As a teacher and writer on economic questions, Sumner accepted the major premises and doctrines of the classical economists, particularly their emphasis upon the necessity for the individual to be able to pursue economic self-interest free from the governmental restraints that had characterized the preceding mercantilist period in English and European history.

Consequently, Sumner was a longtime advocate of a laissez-faire policy for government, a lifelong supporter of the nineteenth-century movement to free international trade from nationalistic tariff restrictions, and a generally consistent opponent of economic monopolies. In seeking freedom of economic action for individuals and nations, Sumner upheld the most basic faith of the founder of classical economics, Adam Smith, who taught that the pursuit of individual self-interest resulted in the greatest good not only for the individual but for society. Sumner understood Smith to mean that the drive for maximum individual profit resulted in maximum production for the entire society.[4] Thus Sumner upheld the value of competition among individuals and nations, competition that he was able to translate rather easily into the social Darwinistic terms of a "struggle for survival" and the "survival of the fittest."

The impress of Malthus and Ricardo upon Sumner's thinking is evident in his concern with struggle in the marketplace and in society. Perhaps no thinkers except Charles Darwin and Herbert Spencer had a more profound influence upon Sumner than Malthus, whose law to the effect that population always tended to grow faster than the food supply, thus causing men to live always under the threat of social distress and famine, was central to Sumner's social thought. To this grim basic assumption Sumner was able readily to add Ricardo's "law of rent," which held that an increasing population forced the use of increasingly poor and less well situated lands, thereby causing both higher rents on the better land and a diminishing return of food from the progressively poorer land. Ricardo thus stressed the limits of nature's provisions rather than its bounty.

Sumner followed Ricardo's lead both in language and in concept by agreeing that nature was "niggardly."

To Sumner, the laws of population and of rent were "cases in which by rare and most admirable acumen powerful thinkers perceived two great laws. . . . We have before us/not special dogmas of political economy, but facts of the widest significance for the whole social development of the race."[5]/The combined impact of the ideas of Malthus and Ricardo upon Sumner's thinking led toward gloomy conclusions and away from Adam Smith's optimistic faith that a benevolent "unseen hand" guided the destinies of mankind. And, yet, as will be seen in the following discussions of Sumner's ideas about sociology, Naturalism, democracy, and capitalism, he was able to conclude, paradoxically, that competitive struggle in the marketplace and in society also had cooperative and even harmonious aspects as men and classes came gradually to recognize their mutual dependency and began to engage in what Sumner the sociologist termed "antagonistic cooperation." Thus, it can be seen that in his economic views and in his later sociological views, as in his early religious views, Sumner envisioned a dialectical alternation between competition and cooperation, between struggle and harmony.

It can also be seen, given Sumner's wide-ranging training, interests, and cast of mind, that his movement from political economy toward sociology possessed a certain inevitability. By the early 1870s, Sumner was well versed in theology, in several languages, in the Classics, in history, and in political science and political economy; and, since at least his graduate study days in Europe, he had been drawn to the new scientific method which seemed to offer the possibility of delineating the laws of society. The study of political economy, at least for the close adherent to classical economics, offered the security of certitude; but to Sumner political economy began also to seem confining. Thus, in 1881, after almost a decade at Yale, he expressed his clearly developed intentions in his essay "Sociology":

It is to the pursuit of sociology and the study of the industrial organization in combination with the other organizations of society that we must look for the more fruitful development of political economy. We are already in such a position with sociology that a person who has gained what we now possess of that science will bring to bear upon economic problems a sounder judgment and a more correct conception of all social relations than a person who may have read a library of the existing treatises on political economy. The essential elements of political economy are only corollaries or special cases of sociological principles.[6]

Although Sumner had felt the impact of several other scholars, the influence of Herbert Spencer had been most responsible for his gradual conversion to the study of sociological principles during the preceding decade, and Sumner's exploration of Spencer's ideas had already embroiled him in a serious controversy at Yale.

## II    *Sociology and Controversy*

As a tutor, Sumner had read but had not been interested in the evolutionism of Spencer's *First Principles*. At Morristown from 1870 to 1872, however, Sumner had read parts of Spencer's *Study of Sociology* which outlined a grand science of society and which, as Sumner wrote later in 1889, brought "into shape the crude notions which had been floating in my head . . . especially since the Oxford days. The conception of society, of social forces, and of the science of society . . . was just the one which I had been groping after."[7] Just as Henry Thomas Buckle's *History of Civilization in England* had stimulated Sumner at Oxford, Spencer stirred even more strongly Sumner's hopes that universal law could be discovered and applied to society.

Within a few years, Sumner revealed in his 1874 review of Spencer's *Descriptive Sociology* and in his own lectures his developing conviction that a social science was possible because history showed that society evolved according to identifiable forces and uniform laws. Convinced that society evolved, Sumner turned to biology; and, as he remembered in 1889, "some time about 1875 or 1876," he was "definitely converted to evolution" by the visual impact of a fossil display that indicated the evolution of the horse. Concurrently, he reviewed Spencer's evolutionary concepts; and then he studied the master, Charles Darwin, and other natural scientists.[8]

From evidence in his writing and from the views of historians of sociology, it appears that Sumner's long-term development of a science of society was most influenced by Darwin's theory of evolution and scientific attitude of mind; by Thomas Robert Malthus's population theory; by Spencer's cosmic vision of the meaning of evolution and its applicability to the study of society; by the German scholar Julius Lippert's use of historical materials to analyze the evolution of culture, as well as by his numerous specific theories on the origin and evolution of social institutions; by the "conflict theory" of the Austrians, Ludwig Gumplowicz and Gustav Ratzenhofer, who stressed the importance of struggles and their consequent resolution among social groups; and by Ratzenhofer's emphasis on social equilibrium that derived from multitudinous conflicting and cooperating "interests" as individuals were impelled by a universal creative force to seek "self-realization." Interestingly, Sumner seems not to have been much influenced by or in touch with other pioneering American sociologists, most of whom, like Sumner, had been drawn to sociology from economics.[9]

This reference to discrete individuals who influenced Sumner's development may be somewhat misleading, however, for he was an omnivorous scholar who responded sensitively to large patterns of nineteenth-century thought and assumptions. These views included the widespread belief that biological, social, and cosmic evolution occurred through progressive stages; that dynamic and organic harmony or equilibrium in society resulted from the rhythmic alternation of conflict and cooperation; and that natural law and scientific methods of study were universally efficacious and beneficent.[10]

In 1882, only a few years after his conversion to Naturalism, Sumner asserted at a farewell dinner for the visiting Herbert Spencer that he could see "no boundaries to the scope of the philosophy of evolution. That philosophy is sure to embrace all the interests of man on this earth. It will be one of its crowning triumphs to bring light and order into the social problems which are of universal bearing. . . . Mr. Spencer is breaking the path for us."[11] Sumner's respect for Spencer remained, but he soon warned in 1886 against believing that "[Auguste] Comte, or Spencer . . . or anybody else has solved the world-problem aright."[12] In the mid-1870s, however, Spencer had been virtually the only authority on sociology; and Sumner had assigned Spencer's *Study of Sociology* to his seniors in 1879. As a result, he had begun, he asserted later, to teach sociology "years before any such attempt was made at any other university in the world."[13]

Then Sumner's trouble began. The source of objections to Spencer's supposed atheism is unclear, but Sumner's opponents on the faculty were apparently involved. His public antagonist was President Porter, who told him late in 1879 that to expose undergraduates to Spencer would harm both them and the college's reputation. As

Yale's president, Porter "presumed" authority to approve texts; he
formally objected to Sumner's choice; and, after Sumner had
rejected Porter's presumption by offering to resign, Porter, according to Sumner, withdrew his formal but not his informal objections.
Sumner's students read Spencer in the spring of 1880, but Porter
informed the Yale College Corporation without Sumner's knowledge that Sumner had agreed to give up the text. When he learned
of this development from Porter several months later and considered
the effects of public controversy past and prospective, Sumner
"suspended" the use of Spencer's text for 1881; but he also clarified
his position in a biting yet controlled statement to the Yale College
Corporation.[14] Sumner first expressed his growing belief "that
sociology was about to do for the social sciences what scientific
method has done for natural and physical science, viz.: rescue them
from arbitrary dogmatism and confusion." Unable to lecture author-
itatively and unwilling to cram and regurgitate some authority, he
had assigned Spencer for two years without ill effect. Indeed, the
assignment had stirred much interest in social science and had
disproved dire predictions that students would be corrupted.

In Sumner's statement to the College Corporation, he rejected
attempts to direct his work and asserted that "Pres. Porter affirms
that sociology is inchoate and tentative. So is psychology; so are
many new developments of physics, biology, and other sciences. To
object to what is inchoate and tentative is to set up a closed canon of
human learning." Sumner asserted that he sought only to develop
sociology, not to attack religion, and that "in my controversy with
Pres. Porter I did not defend agnosticism; I resisted obscurantism."
Sumner noted that Porter himself had used certain of Spencer's
books that Porter apparently believed were not atheistic on the
assumption that this set no precedent, "but I confess that this view
of the matter never suggested itself to me." Sumner denied promising to drop the text, and he denied that the matter was settled
because he considered "that it involves rights and interests which
no honest teacher ever ought to concede." Sumner concluded by
commenting, "I have always considered that the Corporation did
me great honor when they elected me, a young and untried man, to
this important chair. . . . I threw myself into the work of my
department and of the college with all my might. . . . I have refused
(until within six months) to entertain any proposition to go away or
to go into other work. It is impossible, however, for me to submit to
interference in my work."

The Spencer text controversy was notable in the history of academic freedom because Sumner pitted his principles against what he conceived to be an unreasonable and arbitrary administrative position. Although Sumner received considerable support from colleagues and friends, he told a colleague that he felt isolated in the affair and would "eagerly grasp a satisfactory chance to get entirely out of it."[15] Nevertheless, he deliberately threatened to resign; and he told the College Corporation and President Porter that "cases unfortunately happen very often in life where one has to do without the unanimous approval which it would be pleasant to possess. I suppose this is one of those cases." When Sumner later wrote in an undated note that the scientist was sure to be opposed by "vested interests of church and state," he spoke from considerable experience since various interests had pressured him throughout a long career.[16] As a defender of classical economic theory during its declining years and as a student of society's "folkways" and "mores," Sumner knew something of the forces that openly or covertly directed the individual to conform to the mass and to tradition. Sumner was always a consistent and effective advocate for freedom of the mind; for, as he told the initiates of Yale's Sigma Xi Society in 1905, "the only security is the constant practise of critical thinking."[17]

### III   *Scientific Sociology*

Sumner attempted to practice critical thinking—which he characteristically identified as scientific—as he developed his science of society. At the banquet in honor of Herbert Spencer in 1882, Sumner had asserted that, because sociology pursued human welfare, tradition had to abdicate to "true science" and that "a man of good faith may come to the conviction sadly, but he must come to the conviction honestly, that the traditional doctrines and explanations of human life are worthless."[18] As the preceding discussion of Sumner's religious experience indicates, he intended, when he left preaching for Yale in 1872, to reconcile the conflicting claims of science and religion; but he was unable to establish an harmonious balance because his view of science had begun to shift even before 1872. By 1872 he had asserted as a biblical scholar that only scientific method could discover truth; and he had validated science in the name of God. For more than a decade thereafter, he occasionally equated natural and divine law; but his strengthening belief in natural order and in scientific method eventually eliminated any need for higher authority. Indeed, even by 1873, he could tell students that "I have no confidence in any results which are not won by scientific method and I leave aside all traditional and dogmatic systems as scarcely worth noticing."[19] Late in life, he reiterated his consistent theme that science, "our now reigning world philosophy," had "dethroned all the old philosophies."[20]

In his Naturalistic discussions of man's cooperative struggle for existence, Sumner emphasized that, while luck and hard work contributed significantly, men could progress only by employing organized and disciplined intelligence or "science." To Sumner, science was the "knowledge of reality" that scientific men gained by critical, painstaking study; and he believed as early as 1873 that the major early task of science was to free men for knowledge of reality by razing traditional thought systems and by dumping "intellectual rubbish." As a latter-day child of the eighteenth-century Enlightenment, Sumner called up the rays of science to dispel the dark and superstitious past. Sumner thought that science could prevail because the scientist recognized that the universe expressed law and order and that its forces were understandable and at least potentially predictable, except perhaps for ultimate origins and destinies, by the orderly processes of rational intelligence. He wrote most revealingly that science rested on the "faith and assumption" that order prevailed "and [that] . . . the investigation, if pursued strictly according to scientific method, will bring out the truth, so that the mental conception of the man shall correspond exactly to the fact of nature."[21] Although Sumner exchanged faiths, he retained the possibility of human participation in universal order.

As Sumner attempted to develop the meaning of the science of society in universal evolutionary terms, he turned to Herbert Spencer who had gone beyond biology to physics in his formulation of the "Law of the Composition of Forces." For Sumner, Spencer's concept was the "great law of the universe" because it neatly linked motion, evolution, and "harmony" by showing that all organic or inorganic motion resulted from stresses produced by forces in disequilibrium. According to Sumner's understanding of Spencer's law, any system moved constantly from homogeneity toward heterogeneity; but, since any system did so in a continually oscillating or rhythmical pattern because of the pressure of opposing forces, a type of dynamic or working harmony ensued. Since the laws and the forces of social evolution obeyed the Law of the Composition of Forces, they could at least theoretically be understood exactly; and sociology could thus become the science of "the evolution and life of human society."[22]

As a sociologist, Sumner viewed society analogically as an organism whose evolution or adaptation to its life conditions could be traced by studying anthropology and history and whose contemporary life could be analyzed cross-sectionally by statistics. In America, his own sociology pioneered in the use of ethnological materials drawn from history and anthropology. Sumner admitted, however, that sociology could never be as exact as physical science since the nature of society made experimentation and the compilation and interpretation of data difficult. And he recognized that the organic analogy was occasionally inexact, but he also sometimes insisted that biology and sociology were "truly" and "strictly" "cognate" or "parallel" because both biological and social organisms evolved in a struggle for existence that was determined by forces under natural law.[23]

In his seminal article "Sociology" (1881), Sumner "confessed" that sociology was an embryonic science whose only certainty was that "the natural laws of the social order are in their entire character like the laws of physics."[24] That a priori certainty sustained him through thirty years of grinding work, for he wrote in a "Science of Society" manuscript of the early twentieth century that, "since . . . the human race is bound in with all other organisms under laws of life which are a part of the universe, human society is itself only a phenomenon of the universal order. It is a product of forces of nature in which there is no caprice or accident. The forces are acting within conditions which are a part of the whole which is. This whole has been, is, and will be, through some span of time. . . . We live within that span of time in which this universe may be accepted as constant, just as we live within Euclidean space. Such are the bounds of all our sciences."[25] Within the bounds set for it, sociology, like any science, was to serve as a tool in man's search for social welfare. As Sumner wrote in 1881, the "practical utility" of sociology "consists in deriving the rules of right social living from the facts and laws which prevail by nature in the constitution and functions of society."[26]

## IV   *Method and Spirit of Sociology*

Sumner held that sociology could best teach the rules of right living as a science of generalization, for to hope that mere facts would offer a prediction or a law was absurd since such facts were meaningless unless they were organized according to an hypothesis. In a lighter moment, Sumner noticed subjective dangers in interpretation by commenting on Czar Paul of Russia as an historian: "It is true that he was crazy, but we all have our personal limitations, which are most important when we undertake interpretation."[27] Nevertheless, like the Czar, Sumner proposed to forge ahead by collecting facts and generalizing upon them.

To Sumner, sociological method was ideally dialectical in that a round of fact-gathering and hypothesizing was forever succeeded by a new round of fact-gathering and verification or amendment of generalizations. Sumner's sociological method was dialectical because it depended upon a conception of truth that he derived from his understanding of evolutionary theory and scientific method. That conception compelled him to reject dogmatic "Truth" that logical systems created and to believe both that truths were discoverable only by scientific method and that they were relative to time, place, and circumstance. In the oscillation between observation and generalization, Sumner was certain that no place to rest with "great and eternal verities" could ever be found because the method's self-correcting mechanism ensured that scientific findings would continually adapt to the altered conditions that evolution brought. Sumner's rejection of "ancient injunctions" is reminiscent of William James's attack on closed systems, apparently because of their common conception of scientific method. Like the pragmatists, Sumner insisted that truth was in process of becoming and that it would be found not in assertion or intent but in consequences.[28]

As a scientist, Sumner recognized that the complexity of society required that sociology's findings remain tentative even though they might theoretically be mathematically exact. That recognition may have strengthened his conviction that truths were relative and that the scientist always had to probe for certainties on the edges of mystery because "when we go further instead of coming to a precipice or a dead wall we come to a new vista with a new mystery at the end of it. . . . Here assumption and hypothesis give us a standing ground for a new reach out into the unknown."[29] The fact that sociology was newly formed and environed by mysteries, as well as his belief that interferences with a complex society would have unpredictable ramifications, led Sumner to insist that sociology had to be tentative and probing rather than brashly predictive and prescriptive.

For example, he said concerning automobiles that "legislators ought to keep their eye on this thing and *learn* rather than try to control."[30] Sumner deemphasized the positive role of sociology and stressed the limits of science and of man's ability to alter society to his heart's desire because, to a considerable degree, he wished, both as a social commentator and as a path-breaking sociologist, that society could be a laissez-faire laboratory. Although he often recognized that men were creatures of their age and culture, Sumner usually wrote as if his own science were objective and free of national, racial, class, or other biases; but it is evident, especially in view of reform-minded sociologists of his era like Lester Frank Ward or E. A. Ross, that the apparent necessity for Sumner's new science to teach men primarily of limits rather than of possibilities coincided with his nineteenth-century liberalism.[31]

Yet Sumner argued on occasion that men could direct their own destinies within certain limits, as when he asserted early in the twentieth century that "it is quite undeniable that human history has been made by the way in which the men acted in the historical conjunctures."[32] At the appropriate historical conjunctures, for example, laws which forced changes in conduct could induce consequent changes in thought and feeling. The line between Sumner's sense that much of life was determined and his tenuous acceptance of the efficacy of human volition lay in his variant of a not uncommon nineteenth-century assumption that life offered men only a limited number of choices and only at specific times. As an evolutionist, Sumner believed that possibilities of choice and control arose because physical and social environments changed constantly. At the moment when a crucial new conjuncture formed, a choice between forces or a combination of forces was possible which could in time cause great changes, but attempts to alter forces would be futile once they were fully established. Like other Naturalists of his era, Sumner believed that economic choices would be most effective.[33]

Sumner recognized that choices which were beneficial to society depended upon intelligent analysis of alternatives. This understanding led him to view the mind as an extremely important agent despite his understanding that it was a reactive mechanism which served man's innate drives and desires and that forces external to man, as well as the "aleatory element" or chance, narrowly circumscribed the effectiveness of mental activity. The level of individual and social welfare that men gained in the struggle against nature approximated the degree of intelligence as well as the amount of force that they brought to the struggle. As a sociologist, Sumner always taught that civilized man's ability to combine intelligence and power differentiated him from the savage; for the savage lived preeminently by habit and custom.[34] The examination of habit and custom, for which Sumner coined the terms "folkways" and "mores," formed the core of his most important sociological work.

## V    *Folkways*

Sumner's first and last books are anomalous in that the first, *The Books of the Kings*, was a translation of a religious work and the last, *Folkways: A Study of the Sociological Importance of Usages, Manners, Customs, Mores, and Morals*, which appeared in 1906, was his only major sociological study. Upon this last massive book, Sumner's enduring reputation as a scholar and sociologist rests. In 1899 he began to prepare from materials he had collected and used in lectures since the mid-1880s his long-planned "Science of Society," a grand design to show how men sought individual and social welfare as they struggled for existence in a Naturalistic world. One chapter that treated social customs bulged into *Folkways*, the only major division of his master plan that Sumner lived to publish.

*Folkways* focuses on patterns of behavior and belief in social groups in which members are guided by basic and essentially uniform motives as their groups struggle for existence against nature and compete with other groups. According to Sumner's terminology, "folkways" are social habits or customs whereas "mores" are folkways that have passed beyond unconscious usage and have acquired connotations of "rightness" in promoting group welfare. Consequently, mores are sanctioned by "notions" of luck, by demonism, and by religion. Sumner believed that a group's folkways and mores tend toward consistency as its members respond to environmental pressures in the interest of avoiding pain and seeking pleasure, but he believed that folkways and mores may also be modified slightly by the group's best men.[35]

In a long introductory chapter that outlines "fundamental notions," Sumner continued his quest for a scientific framework based on natural laws that would illuminate the meaning of life in human society. Succeeding chapters compile anthropological evidence on such matters as work and wealth, slavery, cannibalism, sex, kinship, sports, and asceticism; and they show how social institutions are shaped and justified by folkways and mores. As Sumner emphasizes in the Preface, "the ethnographical facts which I present are not subsequent justification of generalizations otherwise obtained. They are selections from a great array of facts from which the generalizations were deduced."[36] Thus, Sumner's method was inductive and implicitly scientific.

But exceptions to his objective method and tone appear, especially in the final two chapters. The penultimate chapter discusses history and education from the point of view that historical study should turn from battles and elections to the mores and that education should teach about the influence of mores on individuals and society. The last chapter, "Life Policy: Virtue vs. Success," discusses the subject in various cultures but especially in Western civilization. Naturally, Sumner chooses virtue; and he ends the book—which documents the thesis that "the mores can make anything right and prevent condemnation of anything"—with a warning against "moral anarchy." Implicit in Sumner's warning was his partially developed theory that "mores" were mass-oriented but that "morals" were formed by superior individuals who attempted to purify the mores. As he wrote, "the distillation of morals out of mores is a very slow operation but the product is the best which human society has produced. Mores mean, do as all do. Morals mean that there is such a thing as right. That is, there is a more comprehensive and rational code than what all do."[37] The conclusion of *Folkways* shows clearly that evolutionary Naturalism, upon which the book is based, was never able to prevail over the moralistic impulses that Sumner had learned to respond to long before he had been converted to the philosophy of Spencer and Darwin.

## CHAPTER 5

# *Naturalism*

$\mathbf{A}$S the preceding discussion has suggested, Charles Darwin's theory of biological evolution was central to Sumner's intellectual maturation. Like many thoughtful nineteenth-century Americans, Sumner found himself almost inexorably drawn away from a traditional and stable Christian cosmology. The new world view that Sumner began to develop posited a biological realm and—by analogical extension—a world and even a universe that revealed ceaseless flux under the sole direction of natural forces and laws.

## I  *Preparation for Evolutionism*

When Sumner turned from the church to the academy, he believed that he was taking a positive step to defend religion from the modern tide of science. Yet it seems more than curious coincidence that he was so quickly swept away by evolutionism; for surely such a fundamental conversion was preceded by considerable preparation. Sumner did not accept evolutionary theory until he was approximately thirty-five years old; and, by that time, he had absorbed and partially integrated a large number of intellectual assumptions, many of which he was never to discard and some of which remained at odds with Darwinian theory. Certain of his beliefs that were very much those of modern Western culture, however, ultimately eased his acceptance of evolutionary theory. The impact of Sumner's training as a biblical scientist reveals that, like other educated nineteenth-century Western men, his awed respect for scientific method was fundamental to his conversion to evolutionism.

Sumner's belief as a college student and as a clergyman that growth and improvement resulted from struggle in all of biological and social life was also important to his conversion to evolutionism. The concept of struggle came to be central to Sumner's understanding of the dynamics of evolution just as struggle was central to the intellectual constructs and triumphant experience of modern Western societies. Christian dualism with its stress on constant and climactic battles between good and evil; the capitalism of classical economists like Adam Smith with its central vision that conflict among individuals for profit contributed to social progress; and the Western understanding of the expansion of Europe as a movement of Christianity and Civilization against the forces of paganism, barbarism, and untamed nature were major influences on Sumner. They led to Sumner's assumption that all of life advanced through struggle, and they led ultimately to his acceptance of evolutionism and to the gradual withering away of his religious faith.

Sumner converted to a specific theory of evolution, of course; and, although he was always willing to entertain other hypotheses and to admit readily that Darwinism was imperfect, he continued to believe that Darwin's theory of natural selection was the "best yet."[1] More importantly, once he was converted, he was utterly convinced of the general truth of evolutionism because it seemed to verify earlier discoveries that, for Sumner, were natural laws. For example, he was positive that Darwinian biological theory had incorporated political economy's conception of division of labor and had broadened the "narrower" doctrine of the Reverend Thomas Robert Malthus which held that population always tended to outrun food supply.[2]

## II *Malthusianism*

The economic determinism that was so important to Sumner's Naturalistic thought was especially evident when he discussed the theories of Malthus, for he believed unwaveringly, as he wrote in "Earth Hunger" in 1896, that Malthus had revealed natural law and that "It is this ratio of population to land which determines what are the possibilities of human development."[3] "The grand controlling fact in modern society," Sumner wrote in 1909, "is that the earth is underpopulated on the existing stage of the arts."[4] He long believed that "economic circumstances" "molded" political and social institutions and that "the peace, order, security, and freedom from care of modern civilized life . . . are due at last to economic forces," including preeminently the ratio of population to land.[5]

In an embryonic anticipation of Frederick Jackson Turner's "frontier thesis," Sumner observed as early as 1876 that when underpopulation prevailed—as it had historically in America—

economic conditions were easy, humanitarian and democratic institutions appeared, and optimism flourished; but there was an optimum ratio of population to land. To Sumner, writing in 1883, "it is in the middle range, with enough social pressure to make energy needful, and not enough social pressure to produce despair, that the most progress has been made";[6] and he noted that human beings seemingly required the pressure of necessity to preserve their virtue and productivity and that, when conditions were excessively easy, they turned to vice and sloth. To Sumner, however, there was little likelihood that underpopulation would be endemic because, as Malthus had discerned and Darwin had substantiated, population followed biological law in its constant tendency to outstrip the means of subsistence. Overpopulation was the normal human state—which was to say that struggle, distress, and starvation were normal.

Paradoxically, however, the worst of times were also the best of times for culture and the arts, especially the practical arts; for only the "iron spur" of want or imminent starvation drove men to creativity. If they could not escape harsh social conditions by emigration, want drove men to invent new tools and to develop a more complex, more highly disciplined, and more productive society. Such a society was no equalitarian's Utopia; for there also appeared rigid class lines that tended to aristocracy in the upper strata, exaggerated differences of wealth, and declining interest in humanitarianism and in popular education. But, above all, such a society allowed more men to survive and even to achieve a certain level of comfort than otherwise would have been possible. Men could thus live until biological law led to another wave of overpopulation that would drive naturally slothful men either to advance to a higher stage of civilization or to succumb in the struggle. Unlike Henry George, who had written *Progress and Poverty* in 1879 to show that poverty in an era of progress was socially created, Sumner believed—at least from one perspective—that progress and poverty were inextricably linked by natural law.[7]

## III  *Evolutionary World View*

Given Sumner's preconceptions and especially his Malthusianism, it is understandable that evolutionary theory came to underlie his world view which extended beyond organic life to the "superorganic"—Herbert Spencer's term for society—and ultimately to the entire universe. As an earlier discussion in Chapter 4 has indicated,

Sumner found support for evolutionary theory in the "Law of the Composition of Forces" which taught that forces in disequilibrium caused the interrelated developments of struggle, evolution, and harmony; and this law produced evolution and harmony in the case of organic phenomena when it eliminated organisms that were unfitted for the environment. The "Law of the Composition of Forces" indicated that all motion formed an alternating pattern which was created by intertwining antagonisms and harmonies and that all phenomena alternated between concentration and diffusion. By way of explanation, Sumner wrote, "Why should it seem strange that harmonies and antagonisms coexist when mathematics teach us that harmonies and rhythms arise from [the] composition of antagonistic forces and that varieties of harmony are produced by the number of components and the varieties of their relative duration and ratio to each other."[8] The understanding that all things moved dialectically and endlessly from antagonisms to harmonies to antagonisms was pervasive in Sumner's evolutionary world view.[9]

Sumner's conception of the universal cycle's tendency was not entirely consistent, however, for he alternated between emphasizing that it was ultimately static and that it was to some extent progressive. In society, for example, the cycle of intertwining antagonisms and harmonies derived from alternating conflicts and compromises that individuals and groups experienced as they interacted. Typically, Sumner taught, men learned to subordinate conflicts in order to establish harmony of interests and thus to create a more highly developed and balanced "social organism." In this dialectical process, antagonisms reappeared on each successively higher plane only to be superseded by new and fruitful harmonies. In subscribing to this common nineteenth-century conception of "stages" that rose from barbarism to civilization and in viewing biological developments as moving from protozoa to man, Sumner seemed to believe that evolution was progressive. Yet, he never succumbed to the popular faith in progress without end, and he was at least equally aware of examples of retrogression in biological evolution and in the history of decayed and fallen civilizations. Whether the evolutionary process was finally cyclical or progressive, however, in Sumner's view harmony was never permanent or static; for "all harmonies, of every kind—in music, motion, etc." were "reduceable at last" to the "Law of the Composition of Forces" which required movement.[10]

Finally, it is interesting to notice that the oscillation between antagonisms and harmonies tended toward a mid-point between opposing forces. Sumner's understanding of universal evolutionary processes tended to correspond to his own strong proclivity to seek equilibrium or the Golden Mean in all things.[11] Sumner's discussions of harmony offer an interpretive key to much of his writing and to his social ideal.

## IV   Struggle for Existence

Harmony was the end to be achieved, but in the beginning was conflict. At the base of his system, Sumner established the elementary facts concerning men in a natural world. As natural beings, men had always been and would always be engaged in "the great struggle for existence which dominates all human society" and which, in fact, was "common to all forms of life" because of natural laws of scarcity that Malthus had revealed.[12] In the struggle for existence, men were forced both to wrest raw materials from a "niggardly" nature and to transform them by hard work into usable products. Those who could not or would not obey the discipline of nature succumbed in the struggle. Although Sumner sometimes recognized that nature's method of forcing a struggle for existence was wasteful and that rational man could avoid the struggle and yet improve himself by developing eugenic methods, he more characteristically viewed the struggle as inevitable and self-justifying. For instance, he wrote in an undated note, "The end of life is to live. To maintain the struggle for existence is an end in itself. It defines the end-all and be-all of every living thing to persist and be for the sake of being and exerting its energies in obedience to its own instinct or will."[13] Existence itself tended to become the end of Sumner's Naturalistic ethic.

Sumner believed that, like other organisms, man's opponent in the struggle was nature, but his view of nature was never entirely consistent. In a sermon of 1871 he had seen nature as "only the hem of the robe of God."[14] By 1883, however, writing in *What Social Classes Owe to Each Other*, Sumner had discovered that "God and Nature have ordained the chances and conditions of life on earth once for all."[15] And not long after Sumner had given nature equal billing with God, nature had gone on to claim the stage alone. Always a moralist, who in his religious years had viewed the world as a "moral order," Sumner easily replaced God with nature as man's disciplinarian and judge when he transgressed natural law: "Before the tribunal of nature a man has no more right to life than a rattlesnake; he has no more right to liberty than a wild beast; his right to the pursuit of happiness is nothing but a license to maintain the struggle for existence, if he can find within himself the powers with which to do it."[16] Sumner sometimes presented nature as an impersonal force that felt no human emotions like pity or happiness and that cared not whether men lived or died. Usually, however, he viewed nature as a living force. Sometimes he used the image of nature-as-woman—as a blind but implacable natural Justice or as a passive Earth who "submits to him who most energetically and resolutely assails her. She grants her rewards to the fittest, therefore, without regard to other considerations of any kind."[17] Nature-as-woman, however, was generally less submissive; and, if men wanted her rewards, she had to be assaulted, wrestled with, and conquered. Nature was a "hard mistress" from whom men must "extort" subsistence. Sumner's Naturalism never allowed him to conceive of a harmonious relationship between man and nature.[18]

## V   *The Four Motives and Self-Realization*

In the struggle for existence against nature, man's instinctive purpose was not merely to live but to achieve "self-realization." Like all phenomena—whether organic or inorganic—man served evolution by fulfilling his inherent possibilities. In seeking self-realization, all men acted upon "interests" or "career-interests" that were derived from the four great "motives" of "hunger, sex love, vanity, and ghost fear."[19] By "interest," Sumner referred to all possible physical and social relationships that the individual experienced as he sought self-realization in the interim between his birth and his death. The fundamental relationship between the individual and his environment was, of course, one of a struggle in which the individual might succeed in developing his potential to a high degree but which he ultimately lost in death.[20]

Although the individual was driven by the generalized urge to self-realization, he was impelled specifically by the four great motives. Sumner employed a pleasure-pain psychology according to which the individual acted from interest to satisfy "the four great moving powers of human society" as painlessly or as pleasurably as possible.[21] When Sumner discussed human nature, he usually discovered psychological uniformity among men because man's nature had its roots in "animality" and because the four great motives had sprung from those undiscoverable beginnings: "These four motives are independent of human will. They are original in human nature. Whence they come we never can say. They may be regarded as set by an intelligent creator or as the product of an ultimate force but we meet them as facts of inheritance which we can trace up to no beginning."[22] Primitive men had started with no ideas and no society but, like other animals, with only four "appetites." From those bare beginnings had slowly and painfully evolved all the complexity and sophistication of modern civilized societies.[23]

As a social scientist, Sumner's concern with the normal led him to generalize about human nature wherever it might be found. While a minister, he had believed that although no two individuals were exactly alike, human nature was the same everywhere and always. His later discussions elaborated this unchanging assumption, as when he wrote late in the century that all men were alike within a certain range; that physical, psychological, and social forces were always much the same; and that thinking, feeling, and willing always influenced men in much the same way. Since human nature was uniform and since life conditions varied only within a relatively narrow range, men everywhere tended to develop similar life patterns in their attempts to satisfy the four great motives. Thus, Sumner could believe that a science of society was possible.[24]

For Sumner, a man's primary concern was generally with "self-maintenance" or "self-preservation" because this was "the first instinct of life." Once that interest was satisfied, a man could turn to the other motives. Sumner recognized that such regularities in human reactions were not always easily discernible, however, because the motives acted quite differently on different levels of civilization and because complex and "interlaced" motives were hard to judge as to cause and effect. Furthermore, a man's motives were not always rationally ordered so that, for example, ghost fear might prevail over hunger—which would obviously be to such a person's detriment. Nevertheless, Sumner found that the motive of self-maintenance normally prevailed and that the other motives were generally determined by economic interests.[25]

Not surprisingly, "interests" and "motives" sound much like the "self-interest" of classical economics; for Sumner came to see that the logic of natural law applied universally. Thus, biology had borrowed from political economy the doctrines of division of labor and Malthusianism; and then biology had reciprocated by offering to students of society those concepts of social organization and evolution upon which scientific "societology" could build. As he organized his science of society, Sumner took the four great motives as major divisions of study: "Hunger" became "Self-Maintenance of Society," under which was subsumed the struggle for existence, the "competition of life," "industrial organization," and property. "Love" became "Self-Perpetuation of Society," which included "sex passion," marriage, family, and demography. "Vanity" became "Self-Gratification of Society," which dealt with ornamentation, entertainment, "esthetic effort," and ambition for distinction, power, and glory. "Ghost fear" became the complex category of "Social Reactions," which stemmed from the "mental reactions" of men to environment and experience and which led to the whole "mental outfit" and social organization of mankind. "Ghost fear" led to "goblinism," religion, philosophy, and science, as well as to the "peace-bond," institutions, rights, and governments.[26]

## VI  *Individual and Society*

In the course of human evolution, the interplay of individual interests and motives led to the development of society; but at the center of Sumner's world view was his belief that individual self-realization was natural and imperative. As a sociologist, Sumner was concerned with mass phenomena; and, as a Naturalist, he believed that survival required mutually helpful interaction between the individual and his society. Nevertheless, he tended to conclude that society ultimately existed to further the individual's interests and that the individual ultimately had to serve himself and not society. Sumner's view of universal processes, which was apparently influenced by Austrian sociologist Gustav Ratzenhofer, incorporated individual self-realization as a special case. Sumner held that "all the things we know here in the universe, inorganic or organic, present themselves to us as if surging, moving forward from one stage (birth, beginning, transformation) towards another (death, end, transformation) impelled by a force inherent in each thing which compels it to assimilate or repel all other things with which it has or wins contact [with the purpose of achieving] the utmost realization of its own existence."[27]

Sumner revealed both the profound impact of Naturalism and evolutionism on his thinking and his strong individualism when he asserted that only a world view which focused on self-realization was consonant with evolution. From an evolutionary viewpoint, each individual was born with a certain potential, with a store of energy, and with a series of environmental chances. Thus the individual's only rational and true purpose, so long as his powers endured, was to strive for self-realization to the very limits of his capacities and his "life-conditions." To Sumner, who was a consistent ethnocentric critic of Oriental culture, the alternative was a fatalistic and pessimistic Asian environment in which individual energy was thwarted and in which social inertia prevailed. To Sumner, individual expenditures of energy to meet shifting environmental conditions contributed to universal evolution. Sumner believed that to live and attempt to realize oneself was both a necessity and a duty and that from the individual-environmental relationship a Naturalistic ethic had to be derived with no reference to ultimate ends. Although Sumner's ultimate belief was that man had no end beyond himself, he held that teleologies must be rejected because men were ignorant of origins and ends. The goal of existence for the individual, for society, and for the human race, like that of the universe, was existence itself.[28]

Clearly, according to Sumner's ethic, the individual should not be misled by secondary concern with society, the state, posterity, or "another life." Sumner linked the sociological concept of self-realization and his longstanding libertarianism when he asserted that self-realization meant that man was an end to himself, "and that is individualism." Although generally opposed to natural-rights theories, Sumner implied that natural rights "with liberty" meant that no individual could legitimately be prevented from attempting to realize himself, to acquire property and education, to prolong life, and to seek happiness in the "race of life." Sumner's sociological view of self-realization and his political support of equal opportunity for all to pursue happiness are clearly related. As a libertarian, he approved of a society in which each man was left as free to seek self-realization as his society's necessities allowed.[29]

Sumner's emphasis on the incessant struggle that an individual had to endure to achieve self-realization was, of course, antithetical to self-sacrifice. He held that at birth the individual was a "germ" with an "inherited nature" to develop and that his "life-process" was guided by "instinct or will" through a series of "acts of offense and defense against the environment." If "self-aggrandizement" ceased, the individual lost ground in the struggle, and it therefore seemed clear to Sumner that each individual faced a clear choice: he could choose either life or suicide; that is, he could seek self-realization or he could choose self-sacrifice which was suicidal to the degree that it was undertaken. Sumner claimed, however, to make no pejorative ethical inferences about self-sacrifice. For example, parental sacrifice for children was natural and necessary; from sacrifice came love, which encouraged greater parental sacrifice; and as Sumner testified, the parent-child relationship helped make life worthwhile. Although he excepted the family, Sumner was concerned as a Naturalist to limit self-sacrifice—which indicated a shift from his earlier religious position about charity. Sumner was equally concerned as a Naturalist to emphasize that self-realization and selfishness were not comparable because selfishness represented an excess of self-regarding concern while self-realization could not be linked either to selfishness or altruism. Sumner, who was consistently a supporter of individualism and the social Golden Mean, believed that excessive altruism and excessive selfishness were both "unnatural" and that the search for self-realization was the only natural and rational course for the enlightened individual.[30]

Since the individual inevitably lived in society, it was necessary for Sumner to analyze relationships between the individual and society. Sumner assumed that the entire human race battled the conditions of life while it sought to develop the potential of human nature, but he also recognized that human nature could not be developed collectively. Individual self-realization was impossible, however, except in society and specifically in "high civilization" since "low civilization" tended to crush individuals. Yet even in high civilization, Sumner noted, conflict always occurred between the individual's need for self-realization and the society's drive to coerce and mold individuals. This conflict existed even though it was in society's best interest to develop the individual's highest potential through freedom and education. Society, Sumner insisted, was not an end in itself, but it "exists in order to exist and by cooperative organization to enhance [the] power of its members to persist."[31]

A comparison of Sumner's early and later views of self-realization may both clarify his position and show how it changed. As early as 1869, he held in a sermon that "the life-law of every creature in the universe is to develop fully and harmoniously all the powers with which it is endowed"; and he warned his congregation that each member would have to answer to God for his use of opportunities: "The calling is, there, under Christianity to make the most of one's self, to mount as far as possible toward God."[32] Sumner's view of self-realization changed in that "the calling" was based earlier on duty to God and later upon the individual's duty to follow natural law dictates and to fulfill himself. For Sumner, God was transmuted into Natural Law; and the individual could no longer discover beyond himself a meaning and destiny in the universe, except perhaps in his duty to contribute to universal evolution.

## VII   *Competition of Life*

In barest Naturalistic terms, the source of man's duty was the struggle for existence, in which he sought self-realization as he was impelled by the four great motives. The fundamental or primary struggle was against nature, but the fact that a man did not live alone on a barren planet caused men to come into a secondary conflict with all other organisms and most obviously with one another. Sumner, who called this secondary struggle the "competition of life," noted Darwin's view that competition among organisms was "seasonal, generational or irregularly suspended by 'accident' "; but Sumner stressed that, when it was most intense, the competition of life eliminated least fit organisms and even weaker species. Although he sometimes wrote as if the competition of life occurred between individuals, he usually noted that it appeared only between groups. Men acted according to the dictates of interest in the competition of life, but self-interest had come to be enlightened. Even primitive groups, Sumner discovered, had painfully learned that internecine competition was fruitless and that individuals could best fulfill their long-term goals of self-preservation and self-realization by joining in "antagonistic cooperation" with others even though immediate interests might be compromised. Each man's egoistic interests were best realized in "antagonistic cooperation" with others against the true enemy—nature.[33]

The competition of life, then, led to both conflict and cooperation among men; the latter occurred in the form of an "industrial organization" (much like Adam Smith's "division of labor") that enabled all members of a cooperative group to wrest a better living from nature. But the universal principle of oscillation ensured that struggles among men did not thereby automatically cease. Sumner's belief that cooperative "industrialism" and divisive "militarism" had alternated throughout history from the lowest primitive horde to the highest contemporary societies led him to a central concern with the relationship between human conflict and cooperation in a Naturalistic world.[34]

Perhaps there are always certain difficulties in replacing the intellectual baggage of an outmoded system of faith and understanding. Such was the case at least for Sumner particularly because late-nineteenth-century Naturalism was in an inchoate state; because Sumner was characteristically impelled to seek logic and consistency in the doctrines of his new faith; and because he was reluctant to discard certain of his beliefs that antedated his Naturalism. Partially as a consequence of these difficulties, when Sumner considered the struggle for existence, the competition of life, and "antagonistic cooperation," a fundamental conflict threatened to develop in his thought between his drive to accept the necessities of struggle among living things in a Naturalistic world and his equally deep search for order, peace, and harmony in human society. The tension in Sumner's thought and his concern to alleviate it by creating a consistent world view can be clarified by a more extensive discussion of his adherence to both social Darwinism and "antagonistic cooperation."

## VIII   *Social Darwinism*

Reared as Sumner was in a tradition that sanctioned struggle, one compelling aspect of Darwinism for him was its vision of evolution through conflict, suffering, and death that Herbert Spencer had applied to society even before Darwin had published his theories. It seems inevitable now that Sumner should have become a "social Darwinist" in the sense that Richard Hofstadter uses the term to connote emphasis on struggle from a conservative social position. That Sumner should have been most obviously a social Darwinist when serving as a conservative polemicist is hardly surprising. Perhaps less immediately understandable is that he clung at least as tenaciously to the apparently opposed vision of the cooperative and harmonious possibilities of human existence and that he attempted to demonstrate how both competitive and cooperative urges in human nature could mesh naturally to produce social harmony. Those who have been called social Darwinists, it must be realized, emphasized struggle—especially in the present—but they also tended to look forward to a time of increasing resolution of conflicts, extension of social cooperation, and establishment of equilibrium or harmony within and among social groups. Sumner's Naturalistic science of society postulated a dialectical oscillation between antagonism and cooperation in human affairs that tended toward an ultimate, even if not completely realizable, harmonious state.[35]

Antagonism, of course, had become instinctive in human nature over millennia as individuals had fought to survive against the terrible odds dictated by the fecundity of living things. As Sumner told students in his important introductory lecture on "Sociology" in 1881, "we have already become familiar, in biology, with the transcendental importance of the fact that life on earth must be maintained by a struggle against nature, and also by a competition with other forms of life. In the latter fact biology and sociology touch. Sociology is a science which deals with one range of phenomena produced by the struggle for existence, while biology deals with another."[36] This statement illustrates Sumner's consistent view that social scientists had to develop their discipline "in concord with evolution." Consequently, when he taught over the years that "the law of the survival of the fittest was not made by man and cannot be abrogated by man,"[37] he invited examination of established ideologies and ethics from a harshly Naturalistic and apparently value-free orientation.

To Sumner the law of the survival of the fittest meant merely that organisms which were fitted to survive in an environment did survive while others "perished" or were "eliminated" or "exterminated." The popular attachment of "better" or "worse" to evolution notwithstanding, evolutionary movement was random rather than progressive. To interfere with the law of the survival of the fittest— as did Christianity, humanitarianism, democracy, and socialism— was to ensure (according to Sumner's pet phrase) "that if we do not like the survival of the fittest, we have only one possible alternative, and that is the survival of the unfittest."[38] When humanitarianism and Christianity taught men to pity and to aid the poor and weak, the tramps, the criminals, and the alcoholics; and when democracy and socialism dogmatically sought absolute social equality, they impeded the competition of life and ultimately biological evolution itself. Such interferences not only weakened the strong by inducing them to sacrifice for others but also temporarily strengthened the weak so that they might reproduce inferior characteristics in offspring. Similarly, at the upper end of the social scale "class privileges" and laws of inheritance sometimes allowed offspring of the successful rich to live as parasites, "without requiring of them virtue, wisdom, or ability."[39]

As opposed to "artificial" ethical, ideological, and legal doctoring, Sumner offered nature's remedy: "Nature's remedies against vice are terrible. She removes the victims without pity. A drunkard in the gutter is just where he ought to be, according to the fitness and tendency of things. Nature has set up in him the process of decline and dissolution by which she removes things which have survived their usefulness. Gambling and other less mentionable vices carry their own penalties with them. Now we never can annihilate a penalty. We can only divert it from the head of the man who has incurred it to the heads of others who have not incurred it. A vast amount of 'social reform' consists in just this operation."[40]

Sumner believed that the suffering caused by harsh conditions, as in Ireland, was truly to be lamented; but out of the crucible of that suffering would emerge a fitter remnant to preserve the race: "Now it is terribly true that only the better ones emigrate, and only the better ones among those who remain are capable of having their ambition and energy awakened, but for the rest the solution is famine and death, with a social regeneration through decay and the elimination of that part of the society which is not capable of being restored to health and life."[41] Similar examples could easily be multiplied to show that at times Sumner's social Darwinism was as harsh as the harshest comments of his early inspiration, Herbert Spencer.

Sumner's understanding of evolution as universal was based on the assumption, which he derived from the "Law of the Composition of Forces," that evolution of any kind could proceed only if heterogeneity prevailed. His opposition to deadening equalitarianism, therefore, and his justifications for leaving the drunkard in the gutter and the Irish to survive if they could, depended on his understanding of natural law as favoring social inequality. As Darwin seemed to imply and as Spencer asserted, Sumner argued that the "iron spur" of misery and pain and even death had been and still was necessary for the welfare and progress of the race, and that the alternative which charitable and legal interferences with the law offered was individual and social decay.[42]

Nevertheless, Sumner, whose Naturalism was never entirely consistent, also recognized that, while harsh social conditions selected for survival only the best individuals, they also emphasized society's worst features; and, despite his fascination with the "natural," he persistently called for the extension and protection of civilization which was man's "unnatural" or "artificial" creation. Sumner also occasionally admitted that physical and social evolution were not absolutely "cognate" and that they were different in degree and perhaps in kind. Since men lived in a human and social as well as a physical and natural environment, Darwinism could not conclusively and exactly be applied to society. In that human social environment nature's "wasteful" method had been "superseded" by "devices of culture," by institutions, and by science. Human volition and intelligence had allowed men to move in an oscillating pattern of conflict and harmony up through the stages of civilization in a series of broadening peaceful, legal, and social relationships from the "fist law" of the primitive in-group to modern society. In this evolution, institutions to define and protect civil liberty had replaced violent struggle with lawful competition for material goods through the exercise of such peaceful industrial virtues as hard work and saving. For Sumner, struggle had not been eliminated; it had been transmuted as men rose from barbarism to civilization by acting increasingly on the realization that peaceful competition must replace force in society if the race was to survive and to prevail against nature.[43]

Yet, Sumner the Darwinist continued to fear that the race would not only cease to evolve upward but that it would degenerate under conditions of civilized ease because inferior specimens would survive and breed. To avoid the evils and sufferings of a declining civilization that would consequently fall upon men, Sumner offered two apparently opposed suggestions. As indicated above, one suggestion was to reaffirm the absolute necessity of pain for social advance. Conversely, Sumner followed the logic of his pleasure-pain psychology in the opposite direction when he asserted that, given the expanding opportunities in civilized society, ambition for success and wealth could replace the raw competition of life as the drive behind advances in the "arts" and in industrial power. Hope of future pleasure, Sumner believed, had largely supplanted the pain of immediate distress as the motivating force in high civilization. It was also true that the discovery of new lands, expanded trade, and new inventions had softened the struggle for existence and the competition of life immeasurably for Western men. Men in Western civilization lived in conditions of at least temporary ease so that not all the unfit were eliminated but only those "below some limit of toleration." In civilization, competition was not for existence but for an improved standard of living, for comfort, and even for luxury.[44]

Although he was in one sense a social Darwinist, Sumner consistently expressed his preference for peace over war and for peaceful even though "antagonistic" cooperation over disruptive strife; and, although he perceived an unending oscillation between competition and cooperation, his ideal was peaceful on either side of the alternation. Significantly, he believed that the cooperative aspect was social and that "this raises the plane" from which competition recurred. Sumner's vision of man's history from savagery to civilization was one of an erratic and painful ascent through millennia from conflict toward harmony. As society ascended, he noted "one set of antagonisms after another giving way to the harmonic and rhythmical action of institutions by which rights and interests are adjusted."[45] Of his conception of harmony, he wrote in an early-twentieth-century "Science of Society" manuscript, "The harmony of interests has been a subject of controversy and derision for the reason that (like every other harmony) it arises from a combination of antagonistic forces. If anyone chooses to point to the primary antagonisms he thinks that he has refuted the alleged harmony."[46] Similarly, in *Folkways* he wrote that "it would be an error . . . to suppose that all nature is a chaos of warfare and competition. . . . Competition and combination are two forms of life association which alternate through the whole organic and superorganic domains."[47]

For Sumner, combination, cooperation, and harmony obeyed natural law because they were as "natural" as competition and warfare. Sumner could speak both as a social Darwinist and as an advocate of increasing social harmony with no sense of paradox or inconsistency because of his understanding that evolution of whatever kind occurred through oscillation or alternation. Sumner's understanding of natural law validated both his social Darwinism and his vision of advancing harmony.

## IX   *Antagonistic Cooperation*

Sumner was absolutely certain that advancing harmony in society was promoted by "antagonistic cooperation"—"the combination of two persons or groups to satisfy a great common interest while minor antagonisms of interest which exist between them are suppressed."[48] As a student noted in one of Sumner's lectures, such "antagonistic cooperation" was "nothing but another expression of a universal principle . . . [which was] capable of mathematical expression."[49] Not only the "Law of Composition of Forces" but biology as well revealed "antagonistic cooperation"; for Darwin, Spencer, and others had shown that animals, "social insects," organs, and even cells were both antagonistic and cooperative in their interactions. Like insects and other animals, men cooperated to satisfy the "egoistic" urge to live only because of the competition of life. For Sumner, "egoism" referred to nothing pejorative but only to such acts as "breathing, sleeping, eating" that made "common sense in the struggle for existence."[50] In his religious phase, Sumner had tended to stress love and sacrifice in human relations; but, although as a Naturalist he did not deny their validity, he focused on the necessity of self-regarding characteristics and on the necessary antagonism between individuals because of his assurance, discussed earlier in this chapter, that the alternatives to egoistic "antagonistic cooperation" were debilitating sacrifice of self for others, passive starvation, or suicide.

Despite his Naturalistic stress on individual egoism, however, Sumner always emphasized the precarious but necessary balance between the individual and his society. As a classical economist, Sumner followed Adam Smith in believing that individual egoism and the social good were compatible; as a sociologist, Sumner believed similarly that the individual and his society were "interlaced and inseparable" in a "constant interplay" of "antagonistic cooperation" that was in its best form mutually beneficial. In the "good society," Sumner wrote early in the twentieth century, "the mutual relations of the members is such that they cooperate to the highest realization of all."[51]

Although the origins of "antagonistic cooperation" were lost in prehistory, Sumner hypothesized that the competition of life had forced a man and a woman to come together in order to ease their misery. First the family and then the horde, clan, tribe, and nation had appeared as the benefits of ever-widening cooperation became obvious to men. The process had been dialectical, of course, because even within the clan or the state a constant tendency for harmony to disintegrate had impeded the growth of an expanded system of "antagonistic cooperation" that potentially included all men in a world peace group. Nevertheless, a higher and more sophisticated cooperation had gradually developed. As Sumner believed in 1879, "the tendency is towards an industrial system controlled by a natural cooperation far grander than anybody has ever planned towards a community of interests and welfare . . . and towards a free and peaceful rivalry amongst nations in the arts of civilization."[52]

Although Sumner was uneasy about the new cities that teemed with the immigrant, proletarian, fast-breeding masses, he refused to succumb to nativist scapegoating or to calls for immigrant restriction because he believed that the immigrants' labor was needed for industrial progress and that they would limit family size as they gained a better living standard. "In a generation or two," Sumner told students in 1903, "they will be as good as we are."[53] Even as early as 1879, Sumner had asserted that "the barriers of race, religion, language, and nationality are melting away."[54] Under such conditions, he wrote a decade later, "nationalism becomes an impertinence"; and he often wrote of a "grand and world-wide cooperation" in "the great organized onslaught made by the race on nature." The imagery of an "onslaught" was warlike, but Sumner's intent was pacific; for he also wrote of an economically cooperative "brotherhood of man." Perhaps influenced by Julius Lippert, Sumner even speculated that primitive men had been peaceful and that the competition of life induced by overpopulation had made men warlike. Speculation aside, Sumner knew that history and science taught that men should avoid war and cultivate peace.[55]

Clearly, Sumner was in certain respects a conservative social Darwinist. He was not so merely for rhetorical purposes, although his polemical writing may have stimulated the appeal of images of struggle, suffering, and death; and his social Darwinism did not fade away after its early impact in the 1870s and 1880s. In an early-twentieth-century "Science of Society" manuscript, Sumner argued that men could escape the struggle for existence and the competition of life and yet become strong and efficient if they would "supplant nature's wasteful mechanical method" with a drive to increase luxury and to limit population. But Sumner's proposals to limit population were those of the eugenicist who could contemplate the elimination of idiots and other unfit and infirm persons as possibly preferable for the individual, for society, and for the species.[56]

Nevertheless, Sumner's emphasis on "antagonistic cooperation" clearly modified the harshness of his social views. Although he believed that social cooperation which derived from egoistic interest did not lead to an equalitarian Utopia, his vision of "antagonistic cooperation" was at least tenuously related to his early Christian emphasis on human brotherhood. But his vision was related much more evidently to his later emphasis on the advantages both of peaceful industrialism over militarism and of the world as a peace group bonded by free commerce. In economic terms, Sumner's vision of the good society was of a capitalistic system that encouraged lawful competition and free trade among all men and nations.

Clearly the most important influences on Sumner's thought—Protestant Christianity, classical economics, and contemporary interpretations of the meaning of evolution—stressed not only struggle as the means but also peace and harmony as the desirable ends. Sumner's conception of "antagonistic cooperation" was related, therefore, to his fundamental insistence that in all inorganic, organic, and social phenomena, successively greater harmonies emerged from the dialectical oscillation of antagonisms and harmonies. That insistence implicitly suggests that Sumner believed in progress.

## X   Progress

The idea of progress held Sumner's attention throughout his career, and he always believed that his was a progressive, enlightened age compared to past eras. Nonetheless, he increasingly doubted the wisdom of an unquestioning adherence to the modern faith in progress, and he sought its deeper meanings and ironies. As a college student, Sumner was taught that a "lapse of all mankind" from the progress of civilization and Christianity was "impossible."[57] Similarly, as a young clergyman, his view of progress was virtually indistinguishable from his hope that the Kingdom of God would be established on earth; and he foreshadowed his later acceptance of the theory of evolution when he told parishioners in 1871 that "God's plan in this world is one of growth, development, and progress."[58]

Sumner's early Christian optimism helps to explain why he was inclined to view evolution as progressive when he first accepted the theory in the mid-1870s; but even in his most sanguine moments as a clergyman, Sumner had believed that human progress was slow and erratic; and his stress on the privations and suffering that men had to endure to survive and perhaps to advance increased dramatically as he thought more deeply about the meaning of Darwinism for society. Beginning in the late 1870s, he also made more sophisticated distinctions concerning the possibilities and meaning of progress in the arts, in human nature, and in the universe.

Sumner always held that, historically, progress in the fine arts had been negligible or nonexistent but that progress in the "practical arts" had been clear and irrefutable. As an economic determinist, he defined progress in terms of the increased power over nature that the great modern inventions and discoveries had offered men. Machines, capital formation, more efficient business methods, and the resources and respite from overpopulation offered by the New World had aided men in the grim game of survival. Progress in the practical arts—which had depended partly on chance but primarily on the patient endeavors of men—had given mankind an improved ability to adjust to the ever-changing conditions of existence. Sumner characteristically emphasized that a crucial series of mankind's elite individuals, by hard work, by creative vision, and by the scientific method, had guided the pervasive human urge to self-realization and had thus led men to their present temporary easeful position.

To Sumner, modern society had reached the acme of civilized progress because it had developed the harmonious balance between conflict and combination that "antagonistic cooperation" represented and had thus enabled peaceful industrialism to emerge after ages of militarism. And yet, as Sumner read history, he discerned a striking pattern in the life of nations and societies of growth to maturity and glory followed by decline, decay, and death. This wasteful process, he told his students in 1903, "has been the history of civilization and it certainly is not a very optimistic fact."[59] At times, a deterministic natural cycle seemed at work; but, in other instances, human ills seemed caused directly by weaknesses in human nature.

In his discussions of progress, Sumner was the most ambivalent when he examined human nature. Although he sometimes discovered extremely slight but permanent improvements in the mental and moral characteristics of human nature in the movement of history from the savage to the civilized man, Sumner, like the literary Naturalists of his day, insisted perhaps as often that "the roots of popular error are ineradicable" and that the "brute" in man "may awake again at any time."[60] Sumner's interest in man's atavistic tendencies is also suggested by his library which contained a baker's dozen of Emile Zola's naturalistic novels. Sumner's most optimistic view was that all human progress, especially progress in human nature, had been highly tenuous because it had been subject to human weaknesses and to ubiquitous misfortune. At best, the course of human progress could be graphically illustrated not by a simple upward curve but by vast cycles or spirals that often moved downward and only uncertainly upward. When he was most pessimistic, Sumner believed that history showed only waves in the evolution of human nature and society and that the civilized men who now rode on the crest of a wave of history ignored the inevitable trough ahead. In a 1905 speech about evolution and society to the Yale Anthropology Club, Sumner defined progress as "an inherent stress, strain, or push in the system of nature toward what men like and approve"; and he denied that social evolution was progressive. The natural history of mankind had replaced theology for Sumner, but it showed "no permanent tendency" and was "enthused by no spirit at all."[61]

In approximately the same turn-of-the-century period, Sumner attempted to communicate the magnitude and drama of cosmic evolution in its impact on puny man by using the image of a glacier in a well-written essay that he never published.[62] The essay's objective tone veiled its emotional appeal only lightly as Sumner departed from his usual straightforward style to evoke graphic images—the glacier is like a great dragon; men live and die like soldiers fleeing across a bullet-swept field. Sumner invited the readers of his essay to imagine that they sat above a Swiss mountain valley which an ancient glacier had formed. Sumner observed that when the "teleologist" sees that this now green and fertile valley is the home of a happy human community, he declares that the glaciation process was progressive in preparing a place for man; but he forgets that the glacier may advance again; he ignores the fact of cosmic flux. "We are left face to face," wrote Sumner, "with the great cosmical forces in their everlasting ebb and flow, combination and collision."

To Sumner, the same facts and forces applied to social evolution: "When we talk of progress in history it is like the first view one took of the Swiss valley." In a drama of forces in "heaving and tossing interaction," Sumner wrote,

the men come and go with their interests, hopes, ambitions, pains, toil and suffering, each one bounded by a lifetime within which it seems that all past history was only preparing for it, all present institutions exist to favor it, and all the future depends upon it. The hopes, ambitions and happiness of a man are all selected independently of the seething and tossing of the social forces. . . . In a true scientific view of the matter, a phase of social organization which has lasted long enough to be defined and described like the Assyro-Babylonian, the Classical, the Medieval, the Modern, is only a phase in the everlasting change from what was to what shall be and that change is not polarized between any points of departure and attainment which can be defined or between which any line of rational tendency can be drawn.

Sumner's Naturalistic view of man's quixotic dream of enduring progress in a universe of blind and clashing forces was never better expressed.

Sumner once wrote in an undated note that "at the outermost horizon of our knowledge we try to frame a view of the material universe which shall be true. . . . The view consists of inferences but they are contradictory and we cannot make them into a whole."[63] Nevertheless, he consistently sought to see things as whole with the insights that evolution offered; but, in the universal evolutionary process, he found no beneficent force that was intent upon shaping the cosmos to suit man's ends as did many of his contemporaries and as he had found earlier in Providential design. Less explicitly than his contemporary, Henry Adams, but unlike most Americans of his day, Sumner began to consider seriously the implications of the Second Law of Thermodynamics which taught him that the universe moved toward complete homogeneity, or entropy; and he finally believed that evolution at any level required decay and dissolution as well as progress.

In a turn-of-the-century manuscript entitled "Progress," he stated that "the outcome of the whole universe may be, so far as we can find out, another nebulous mass like the one from which, so far as we can find out, it came. . . . The whole existence of the earth presents itself as a wave which begins at a zero line[,] moves through a maximum and returns to the zero line. It is, however, interrupted by minor wave motions of rise and fall and the view of men, even if it includes all history, encompasses but the minor fluctuations on a certain extent of the great wave of earth existence. . . . Even then it will perhaps all recommence and run the same course again." Progress, Sumner wrote, is like a man who, having lain a long time on a rock, turns and feels much better; but soon the pain begins again.[64]

As Sumner had realized in the later stages of his religious phase in 1873, men were alone on their world island, "shut out from the inhabitants, if there be any, of any other planet . . . shut up to a common lot and a common destiny."[65] By the late nineteenth century, Sumner believed that man's lonely struggle would end only when an altered "conjuncture" at some point in the endless reaches of time eliminated the play of human force. The human destiny, he wrote, "is a zero undoubtedly."[66] Sumner stressed repeatedly that "the evolution philosophy has won dominion over the thinking of our age. . . . If this view is correct, the moral sense of human existence must lie in it and ethical relations must be deduced from it."[67] Yet, when he found that, so far as men could tell, there was nothing ethical or teleological in the evolutionary process, he was

forced to rely on the resources of men to make their own meaning
for existence. The intensity of Sumner's Naturalistic world view was
revealed in his existentialist perception that men lived for a moment
within some great cycle of the universe in which they were without
external support or direction, were cast upon their own intellectual
and moral resources, and were forced to seek their own duty and
destiny.

## CHAPTER 6

# *Democracy*

ALTHOUGH Sumner's Naturalism offered him a means of interpreting the cosmos, it also helped him in his immediate concern to define the meaning of America. As a political economist, historian, and sociologist, Sumner regarded America as a momentous social experiment that had resulted in democracy. He attempted, as behooved a social scientist, to delineate the objective factors in the American experience that had produced or helped clarify the meaning of democracy. Sumner's analysis of social class in America best clarifies his understanding of democratic society as well as his highly subjective and moralistic class loyalties.

### I  *Social Class Analysis*

When Sumner examined American social classes, he faced a largely unconscious dilemma because he approached classes from two opposed points of view. As a dedicated Naturalist, he viewed social classes as the ever-changing products of society's search for sustenance; but his subjective preferences for a middle-class and even democratic society that he feared might be destroyed always impinged on his attempts to describe classes objectively. Sumner assumed that, unless government or other forces interfered, classes formed naturally as individuals rose or fell to their level of "capability" in the competition of life; that the "societal value" of a class was determined by its mental, moral, economic, and physical characteristics; and that such characteristics tended to be consistently strong or weak within a given class. Although Sumner developed and refined his sociological analysis of class over many years, his views hardly changed throughout his career. Although he analyzed numerous classes and subclasses, his discussions of the masses, the elite, and the middle class best clarify his views of democratic government and society.[1]

95

## II  *Masses*

In *Folkways*, influenced by the German anthropologist Otto Ammon's work in statistical probability, Sumner assumed that, in a given population, a series of classes or social strata which were defined by his criterion of social value would fit into a curve of probable error. According to his graphic illustration, at the "bottom" of the curve were the "three d's"—the "dependent, defective, and delinquent" classes—which were a stratum of "societal waste" or the "dregs of society." Next on the curve was the "proletariat" class, which included those who were not "at the moment" dependent on society or outlaws in it, and slightly above the proletariat on the scale of social value were the "unskilled and illiterate" classes. At the center of Sumner's curve and at the core of society were the masses, whose members tended to live instinctive, unreasoning lives although they could sometimes be led to imitate the creative and innovating classes; but the masses ultimately determined and conserved society's folkways and mores. The masses were especially important because they had increasing political control in modern democracy and could thereby shape modern society. As Sumner bluntly described the masses, "they are fate."[2]

To Sumner, the masses were being gradually but perceptibly elevated by modern education and science and by the ambition which resulted from opportunities that modern discoveries and inventions offered. Thus, in *Folkways*, he skewed Ammon's curve of probable error by showing more of the masses above the dead-center level of "Mediocrity" than below; and he asserted that this rising trend of the masses was "the great safety of democracy." Despite sanguine expressions, however, Sumner was haunted by specters from both past and future; for the logic of evolutionary theory and demographic history impelled him to conclude that harsh conditions would once again fall upon mankind. When he thought in such terms, Sumner stressed man's unchanging psychological uniformity and his atavistic tendency to revert to superstition and savagery. For example, he ended a lecture in 1903 by noting that English colonists had adopted the Indian practice of scalping. Like all social phenomena, human nature moved as the tides of great forces ebbed and flowed; but its level remained constant, especially, Sumner seemed to believe, among society's lower strata. Fearing anarchism, socialism, and Populism, Sumner agreed with the British historian William Lecky that, in the present and in the future, "superstition" would infiltrate political life.[3]

When Sumner attacked unsavory democratic tendencies, he often referred to the masses, which he also called the demos or the class of numbers, as a monolithic stratum; but he occasionally viewed the masses as composed of substrata of varying social value. To Sumner, the differences between the upper and lower substrata of the masses might be very great indeed since the lower touched the unskilled and illiterate stratum and the higher touched the stratum of talent. When the masses were assumed to be multiform, it obviously mattered greatly "which part of the masses sways their own number." In *Folkways* Sumner suggested that, in democracy, "the great central section of the masses" swayed the entire stratum; but it did so only as it, in turn, was led by opinion-makers. The crucial question to Sumner was whether the masses would be led by demagogues or by a disinterested elite.[4]

## III   *Elite*

Although Sumner often discussed society's elite, he did not list this group as a social class on the *Folkways* curve of probable error, a fact that requires explanation. Sumner's interest in class was paralleled and probably stimulated by his concern that society be a commonwealth—that narrow class interest be subordinated to the common good—and this concern was related to his conservative and Naturalistic understanding that a society had to be a cooperative organism in order to prosper. Sumner's concept of "antagonistic cooperation" expressed his desire for a commonwealth because it blurred social divisions and class conflict and stressed the benefits of social cooperation. Paradoxically, Sumner wished both that society could be composed of functional "classes" or "organs" and that it could be rid of class consciousness and the dangers of social polarization. Ideally, society should function in organic unity while its organs, like Sumner's elite, acted psychologically as nonclasses.[5]

While the chief duties of Sumner's ideal elite were to form society's thought, to organize its activities, and to act as its critics, the "elite" was not equated with the "ruling class" but was referred to as the "best" men. Not long after Sumner returned to Yale, he announced to students in 1873 that "we must mold public opinion— this new power until recently unknown as a social force, but now seen to be the great engine which controls the whole." "I desire," he continued, "to . . . furnish the country with citizens of sterling worth, and to give to the professions men whose public influence will tell in the cause of liberty, industry, and honesty."[6] Some years later, the *New York Times* reported that Sumner had said "that he was not a politician, and he did not care how the people of the United States voted at any particular election. He spoke as a scientific man, and as a citizen desiring to have the right prevail."[7] Sumner, like other members of the elite, viewed himself as a responsible, disinterested, scientific citizen whose concern for the common good raised him above petty politics. In general, Sumner's elite expressed the same character traits that he either possessed or desired.

According to Sumner's understanding, the masses of men unthinkingly obeyed their society's folkways and mores; but the morally courageous, talented, and scientifically trained members of the elite had managed to free themselves slightly from the social environment; had become cosmopolitan and catholic in their interests and sympathies; and thus had been able to lead mankind toward whatever progress it had made. A complicated bond, which was almost a type of "antagonistic cooperation," united the elite and the masses, for the elite thinkers were the innovators—society's yeast—while the lumpish masses ensured social continuity. The best men could suggest and guide social progress, but the nature of the masses ensured that changes could not be forced; the elite must follow or slightly anticipate changes in the mores which resulted from great economic developments that moved the masses. Sumner's judgment varied as to the extent to which an elite could influence society, but he consistently maintained that its work could be particularly fruitful if it concentrated on the more enlightened upper levels of the masses.[8]

## IV    *Middle Class*

Like his elite, Sumner's "middle class" does not appear on the *Folkways* curve of probable error and for the same reason that it represented his ideal. Despite his use of the term, Sumner clearly regarded the "middle class" as not in the "middle" but as in the upper strata of the masses. "The upper part. . . " Sumner wrote in *Folkways*, "is made up of the strata which possess comfort without luxury, but also culture, intelligence, and the best family mores. They are generally disciplined classes, with strong moral sense, public spirit, and sense of responsibility."[9] Sumner regularly held that the most valuable individuals and classes possessed a harmonious combination of social, mental, and moral characteristics, a position which was reflected in his belief that the middle class was the most valuable socially. Sumner held that, occupationally, members of the middle class were widely distributed but that they had "earned and saved" and probably had acquired property. In achieving "comfort without luxury" by exercising the industrial virtues, the middle class differed from the poor and sometimes from the rich. Although the middle class did not rank mentally with the strata of genius or high talent, education and training had enabled its members to make significant social contributions.[10]

The middle class rated highest when Sumner judged classes by a moral criterion, for its members possessed the best public and private mores, and they inculcated them in its offspring. In these respects, the middle class differed from both the upper and the lower classes. Although Sumner wished to prevent imbalances at either end of the social spectrum, the economic and moral facts of life were such, he believed, that the rich could afford large families while the poor were too irresponsible to limit their progeny. Many members of the middle class, given their high sense of social and family responsibility combined with inadequate income, inevitably remained celibate or married late and had small families. "It is among the middle classes that we find the *best parents*," one of Sumner's students wrote in his notebook during a lecture of 1903, which explained that, since wealthy parents had many interests, they often abandoned their offspring to a nurse: "This is not a good way to bring up children. . . . It is a pity to find that the propagation of society is kept up from the top and from the bottom and not from the middle classes."[11] Particularly in his later years, Sumner was gloomy; for, as he wrote early in the twentieth-century, society's "strength, vigor, and hope are in the middle."[12]

Although Sumner was a Naturalist, his belief that civilization was an unnatural creation of "antagonistic cooperation" and that civilized men moved precariously above the abyss of miserable conditions helps to explain his elevation of the elite, his defense of the middle class, and his fear of drastic social change. Like many contemporaries of a wide range of political persuasions, class war and social polarization were anathema to Sumner; but, he often pessimistically viewed society as composed primarily of warring factions and as inevitably tending to polarize. Sumner held that all classes, except his ideal of the middle class and the elite, behaved as greedy interest groups which sought to devour society's product for themselves. And he believed that a broad middle class could serve as a crucial mediator that would reduce hatred between social polarities, but he was also certain that the noninterested middle class would perennially be threatened with extinction as it stood guard over American democracy between a "proud and powerful plutocracy" and a "hungry proletariat."[13]

The middle-class individual, whom Sumner immortalized as the "Forgotten Man" who paid with his industry for the indolence of others, stood between conflicting classes because he lacked the cohesive principle of class interest. One could suggest parenthetically that the Forgotten Man may have lacked organization more than interest, but Sumner's dilemma was that he could not urge the Forgotten Man to organize in the social struggle because to do so would have violated his ideology of the independent individual who was "subject to no man" and to no organization and who was "in a certain sense, an isolated man."[14] Caught between the reality of organized class conflict and the ideal of the free individual, Sumner could only castigate interest groups and bemoan the fate of the Forgotten Man of the middle class.

## V    *Elite and Middle Class*

Despite surface differences, Sumner's elite and his middle class were virtually identical when he judged them by the standard of social value. Economically, both groups fell in the middle range; but the members of the elite were primarily professionals, public servants, or academicians; and Sumner made it clear that the elite individuals who wrote books could not be judged by everyday economic standards. Mentally, the elite and the middle class did not differ radically because extremely high intelligence was not a prerequisite for even the best men. Sumner emphasized that training, experience, and particularly the scientific attitude were more important than extremely high intelligence. Both classes received Sumner's highest moral rating as responsible citizens and as noninterest groups. The circle of responsibility tended to be smaller for the middle-class man since it included chiefly his family, but he did his duty and sought no favors in society. The member of the elite had broadened his understanding and sense of responsibility to encompass all of society. Finally, each group was of the highest social value because the standard of a harmonious combination of factors applied to each almost equally well. When one judges the elite and the middle class by Sumner's belief that the most valuable members of society possessed "talent, practical sense, industry, perseverance, and moral principle," one discovers that he scarcely differentiated between the two groups except in their level of talents because both groups, as well as the standards by which Sumner judged them, were related ideals.[15]

The relationships between the elite and the middle class were comparable to those between a wise teacher and a bright pupil, for the prime function of the elite was to form and guide public opinion. Not all members of the masses—and certainly not the social dregs below the masses—could grasp and accept intelligent views. Consequently, if the elite were not to form an isolated clique, it would have to appeal to the upper strata of the masses, to the intelligent and educated middle class. When a cooperative relationship between the two groups could be formed, all of democratic society would benefit.

## VI    *Descriptive Analysis of Democracy*

As in his discussions of social class, Sumner was unable to maintain a uniformly dispassionate and scientific attitude toward democracy. Consequently, the following discussion illustrates that, even though Sumner became somewhat more critical of democracy as he fell away from religion into Naturalism, he mingled descriptive, pejorative, and normative characterizations of democracy throughout his career. When he spoke descriptively as a Naturalist, Sumner regarded American democracy as the inevitable but temporary product of a combination of favorable demographic conditions and of technological development. The discovery of the New World had offered men a favorable but ephemeral ratio of population to land with the result that "democratic tendencies" had swept aside "every constitutional restraint" in their path.[16] But Sumner warned optimists that the prevailing conditions of "progress and modern enlightenment and democracy and the happiness of the masses" would change as overpopulation occurred.

As a Naturalist, he emphasized the urgent necessity of industrial development; and he admitted that the democratic condition was less precarious than it otherwise would have been because industrial technology had been developed. Nevertheless, although Sumner believed that industrialization would elevate civilization somewhat, his expectations about the results of machine culture were severely limited because he feared that the population would use good times to breed even more prolifically. "We find ourselves," Sumner wrote in an undated manuscript early in the twentieth century, "squirming in the grasp of forces which through all changes remain equally undiminished."[17]

As in the case of other socioeconomic processes, Sumner envisioned repeated alternations as first overpopulation and then higher civilization prevailed. Because the pattern was cyclical, the contest between civilization and overpopulation would continue so long as the race existed. It was true, of course, that men had followed something like a spiral course in rising through the stages of civilization, but even the highest stage possessed no guarantees. Indeed, Sumner believed that civilization would probably decline, democracy would pass away, and aristocracy would reappear. Sumner taught that "there are no dogmatic propositions of political philosophy which are universally and always true; there are views which prevail, at a time, for a while, and then fade away and give place to other views."[18]

But the wave of the present and the foreseeable future in America, Sumner believed, was all toward democracy. A century earlier, "a kind of democratic revolution" had paralleled the fight with England; and the conservatism of the Constitution makers' puny devices like the electoral college had not been able to withstand the democratic trend. In his *Jackson*, Sumner argued that democracy, the rising tide of history, would inevitably and increasingly dominate not only American but world society. Democracy encircled the globe while oligarchic and aristocratic forms receded.[19]

## VII   *Pejorative Analysis of Democracy*

Sumner consistently maintained that, because the democratic tide was inevitable, there could be no sweeping back the sea, even if one desired to do so. Late in the nineteenth century Sumner wrote that the masses, which he personified as the working man, found that economic forces were increasingly "throwing the world into his hand." The serious question, wrote Sumner, is "what will [he] do with it and us?"[20]

To Sumner, foreseeable prospects were not bright because, as *Folkways* taught, the masses were the core of society that, especially in democracy, determined not only its mores but all aspects of the social process. As Sumner examined the nature of the masses in democracy, he discovered that democracy atomized society and that the community thus tended to be powerless because the masses were disorganized. Since the success of any social movement depended upon the ability of leaders to rise and form new concatenations of social atoms, the most pressing question for a society "resolved into its constituent atoms" was "under what forces, and upon what nuclei, it will crystallize into new forms."[21]

Socialism always appeared to Sumner as among the most dangerous forces that might organize the social atoms in American
democracy. His early training in orthodox political and economic
theory, bolstered by his religious education, ensured his consistent
opposition to socialism. In a sermon of 1871, Sumner upheld the
Christian doctrine of the brotherhood of man but warned his
parishioners that Socialist movements had taken this doctrine and
had made it the central tenet of their new religion. "In this view,"
Sumner continued, "we have the doctrine of the brotherhood of
man pushed to an absurdity. The individual, with his rights and
duties, is lost sight of entirely."[22] Here in its barest form was
Sumner's concept of a Golden Mean that had to be maintained
between the rights and duties of the individual and of society.
Excessive individualism led to anarchism, but excessive attention to
the demands of society led to socialism. Sumner later incorporated
his view of the necessary balance between the individual and society
into his Naturalistic evolutionary philosophy.

Socialistic schemes might tout the brotherhood of man, Sumner
believed, but in practice they were "without exception appeals to
the greed of the masses, for . . . taking from those who have and
giving to them that have not."[23] In 1885, Sumner repeated a
definition that he often used: "Socialism is any device or doctrine
whose aim is to save individuals from any of the difficulties or
hardships of the struggle for existence and the competition of life by
the intervention of 'the State.' "[24] When Socialists turned to government for help, Sumner taught not only that they rejected the
doctrine of laissez-faire but that they necessarily subverted private
property, the institution of the family, and, indeed, the entire
structure of the ideal competitive system of capitalism that he
upheld rigorously.

To counter the grave threat of socialism, Sumner sometimes
attacked it straightforwardly; but he often used the weapon of
ridicule and satire. Whatever his rhetorical technique, however,
Sumner took the position that he was a hardheaded realist, a social
scientist who wrote to correct the notions of generally foolish and
simple-minded but sometimes dangerous Utopians. These were
latter-day dreamers who in former eras had yearned for a lost
Golden Age or, if they were religious, had eagerly awaited the
Millennium. "Romancers soar above the realities of life," Sumner
wrote in 1878, "create ideals, assume impossible means and combinations, and so excite aspirations and wishes which fall back upon

themselves, only to make life seem more dreary and hopeless than before. Social science cannot compete on this field, and, since utopias have gone out of fashion, it does not aim to."[25]

The subject matter of social science is exceedingly difficult and complex, Sumner wrote in his essay "Sociology" in 1881; yet "the utopians and socialists make easy work of the complicated phenomena with which sociology has to deal. These persons, vexed with the intricacies of social problems and revolting against the facts of the social order, take upon themselves the task of inventing a new and better world. They brush away all which troubles us men and create a world free from annoying limitations and conditions—in their imagination."[26] "That is why it is true," Sumner wrote years later in the early twentieth century, "although socialists are annoyed by the assertion, that socialism is not a subject for discussion by serious students of the science of society."[27]

Although Sumner spent relatively little time and space commenting on individual Socialists, Utopians, and radical reformers, preferring to warn generally against the dangerous implications of socialistic schemes, he did sometimes criticize leading advocates of radical social reform. Henry George, economist, reformer, and author of an 1879 book on *Progress and Poverty*, was probably most often Sumner's target. George was no Socialist in ordinary terms, but Sumner's definition cast a broad net. After George had noted the paradox in America of increasing poverty in the midst of increasing wealth, he concluded that the central cause of poverty and distress was speculation in land and monopoly control of the land and its income by private owners. According to George's analysis, appreciating land values in America, caused by the growth and labor of the entire society, brought rewards to private owners of land in the form of unearned increment in rents and land values. His solution was to allow landowners to retain both their titles and the income from such improvements to the land as buildings but to lay a tax upon the entire unearned increment. Both capital and labor, freed from burdensome taxes by this "Single Tax" upon land, would flourish, poverty would disappear, and the entire society would enjoy unprecedented well-being.[28]

As a result of the popular success of *Progress and Poverty*, George became a hero among social reformers, and numerous Single Tax movements and communities flourished for a number of years in America and elsewhere. But to Sumner, writing in 1881, both George's economic notions and his understanding of historical and political realities were inadequate because America's abundant land resources kept rents too low to allow a Single Tax to succeed and because small landowners, who were prepared to defend property rights, held political power.[29] Sumner admitted late in the century that rising land values in America had resulted from immigration, but he ignored the issue of land speculation that *Progress and Poverty* had raised when he argued that immigrants paid higher land prices because the earlier settlers had to be rewarded for the hardships they had endured while improving the land.[30] Sumner judged that George's "felicity of expression far surpasses his power of analysis"[31] and that "crank legislation according to a Henry George or some other half-educated apostle of the millennium" imperiled property rights.[32]

Edward Bellamy, the journalist and writer whose Utopian *Looking Backward, 2000–1887* (1888) and its sequel, *Equality* (1897), made him the center of an important "Nationalist" movement to reform politics and society in America and elsewhere, was somewhat easier for Sumner to refute than George had been. Bellamy was appalled by the greed and human degradation that he saw in the capitalistic system as America underwent the industrial revolution of the late-nineteenth century. Consequently, he organized *Looking Backward* so that criticism of the evil present was juxtaposed to scenes from the future good society.

Bellamy's social criticism and his writing are most effective when the book's leading character, Julian West, descends into the hell of Boston's working class and reemerges to say that he has seen "Humanity hanging on a cross."[33] By contrast, in the good society of the year 2000, humanity has ascended to an indeed Utopian level of material and spiritual development because public opinion has gradually changed so that it has become possible to replace capitalism with state socialism. Thus Bellamy presents the environmentalist argument that once the means of production and distribution have been taken from private hands and made the property of all, once cooperation in the "industrial army" has partially replaced individualistic competition, and once material plenty has eradicated poverty, the basic goodness in human nature will be free to flourish and a renaissance of human relations, of culture, and indeed of all aspects of life, will occur in America and begin to spread through the world.

Thousands found *Looking Backward* a moving book, but Sumner was apparently not moved. Little appeared in his writings in direct response to Bellamy, except for a few pages in an essay of 1894 significantly titled "The Absurd Effort to Make the World Over" which stated that social reformers as a class tended to base their arguments upon faulty information and faulty understanding of social facts as well as upon idealistic and unverifiable dogmas. As for Bellamy, Sumner took the position that democracy in America— government by the masses—had been responsible for the numerous ills that "Mr. Bellamy and his comrades in opinion see in our present social state, and it is difficult to see the grounds of asking us to intrust it also with industry."[34]

Furthermore, wrote Sumner, Mr. Bellamy may assert that the problem with democracy is that "it has been infected with industrialism (capitalism); but in that case he must widen the scope of his proposition and undertake to purify democracy before turning industry over to it. The socialists generally seem to think that they make their undertakings easier when they widen their scope, and make them easiest when they propose to remake everything; but in truth social tasks increase in difficulty in an enormous ratio as they are widened in scope."[35] Finally, Sumner wrote, still implicitly criticizing Bellamy's Utopia,

Can anyone imagine that the masterfulness, the overbearing disposition, the greed of gain, and the ruthlessness in methods, which are the faults of the master of industry at his worst, would cease when he was a functionary of the State, which had relieved him of risk and endowed him with authority? Can anyone imagine that politicians would no longer be corruptly fond of money, intriguing, and crafty when they were charged, not only with patronage and government contracts, but also with factories, stores, ships, and railroads? Could we expect anything except that, when the politician and the master of industry were joined in one, we should have the vices of both unchecked by the restraints of either? In any socialistic state there will be one set of positions which will offer chances of wealth beyond the wildest dreams of avarice; *viz.*, on the governing committees.[36]

It is hardly surprising that Sumner paid little more attention to Bellamy, for the author of *Looking Backward*, unlike Henry George, made no pretense of being an expert in political economy when he wrote a book that was avowedly Utopian–and about that genre, Sumner insisted, the serious scientist of society could have little to say. More importantly, as the popularity of *Looking Backward* and the Nationalist movement gained momentum in the 1890s, Sumner both broke down in health and turned increasingly to sociological research, with the consequence that his writing on contemporary American issues lessened dramatically. During the presidential campaign of 1896, he did write several articles from an orthodox gold standard position which attacked the Populistic plank of the Democratic party platform that called for the free and unlimited coinage of silver. Although most of Sumner's discussion dwelt on the technical arguments of political economy, he also suggested that Populistic debtor farmers were gamblers who would have accepted winnings but who now wanted someone else to pay their losses; and he intimated that the Democratic party's candidate, William Jennings Bryan, was a demagogue.[37]

A major exception to Sumner's tendency in his later years to withdraw from public controversy occurred in 1904 when he attacked Upton Sinclair's socialistic ideas. Among the radical reformers that Sumner criticized, Sinclair was one of few to whom Sumner devoted an entire essay; but he did so only because the editors of *Collier's Weekly* recruited him to respond to an article by Sinclair.[38] Although the exchange was lively, it elicited no arguments from Sumner that he had not made often before against socialism. Perhaps it is most important to recognize that, in attacking socialism through Upton Sinclair, Sumner's perennial fear that the masses in democracy would seize upon socialism as a panacea for the ills of life led him, as always, to stress the need in democracy for laws and the Constitution.

The problem of how and by what forces the democratic masses would be organized became worse for Sumner when he defined democracy as a system moved solely by majority will. Extreme democracy abhorred laws, institutions, and constitutions because they inhibited the willful majority. At its worst, "democracy has no history, no past, and no future. It lives and acts from day to day. Democracy can make no State, for it has no coherence, no unity, no consistent purpose, and no organization."[39] Sumner was glad in 1882 that the country had a constitutional system and was not an "unlimited and ever-changing democracy." Sumner's opposition to democracy and his sense of the gulf between the elite and the masses was heightened by his social Darwinism and by his penchant for dramatic rhetoric. At times he virtually echoed the German philosopher Friedrich Nietzsche by asserting that, although democratic society was theoretically equalitarian, the weak and inferior actually exploited the strong and superior. Sumner opposed such an injustice, but he could never escape the ideal of a responsible elite that served an atomized, democratic society. He relieved the consequent logical tension when he made a subtle distinction between the elite as exploited and the elite as leading in society's struggle for existence and for the achievement of a higher civilization.[40]

Perhaps partially because of his evolutionist emphasis upon inevitable social change, many of Sumner's attitudes were influenced by his loyalty to conditions that he felt were unfortunately changing. His fear and nostalgia were evident when he argued that "republican" government was falling before democracy or that democracy was threatened by "social democracy." Sumner expressed his pessimism in 1886 when he wrote that "constitutional liberty . . . stands just now as a happy phase of civil institutions which we have been able to realize for a moment in the interval between the downfall of aristocracy and the rise of democracy."[41] He feared the rise of democracy itself, for he was also certain that it would prepare the way for socialism and that socialism would inevitably give way to plutocracy. To Sumner, there would be little from which to choose among the evils of each.[42]

A key error of democracy, Sumner believed, was that it deified majority will. Sumner consistently opposed the claim by "numbers" of a divine right to rule when he asserted that majority rule was merely an expedient device for governing society because political unanimity was normally impossible to obtain. But, like all sovereigns, the majority was likely to become despotic. To ensure justice and civil liberty for all citizens, especially minorities, it was necessary to establish institutional checks on the democratic majority. This would be difficult, Sumner wrote in 1880, for it required as much "moral courage" to "beard King Majority as . . . King Caesar."[43]

Another major weakness of majority rule was that it assumed equality of political judgment among men, but such a dogma was a "corruption of democracy." Sumner always insisted that the true democratic (actually republican) dogma required citizens to rely on the trained and superior representative; but he discovered early in the twentieth century that his fears of the degradation of democracy had been realized. As a latter-day advocate of republican political theory, Sumner believed that he had advanced beyond the understanding of the eighteenth-century fathers of republican government who had expected that the people would choose only the best representatives. Experience had shown otherwise, for the people's legislatures, which were mediocre or worse, either succumbed before the attacks of plutocratic special interests or cooperated eagerly with them. It would not do to argue that the politicians controlled the people: "It is true, but it is a fatal answer. What shall be said of an oracle which pleads that somebody deceived it?"[44] The assumption that all men were equal in political judgment, Sumner always taught, ensured the loss of self-government and the domination of society by plutocracy.

Still another major—and paradoxical—weakness of democracy was that it would become too strong—would become a weapon of overwhelming power wielded by the masses. The consequence would inevitably be to create antagonisms between the masses and the better classes. Just as faction had been one of the gravest threats to a republic for Alexander Hamilton, to Sumner one of the worst enemies of democracy was faction; and he warned that greed fed factions in a democracy. Sumner stressed unbending devotion to the industrial virtues of hard work and to saving so much that he might have seemed to appeal to avarice; but he never forgot to say, if only parenthetically, that wealth-getting should serve merely as a foundation for higher values. When Sumner secularized a religious work ethic, he was enabled to distinguish between natural and unnatural methods of gaining wealth. Consequently, he could assert that greedy class government resulted in democracy when the masses learned that they could not successfully compete with talent in the economic struggle. Class war ensued as honest business was forced to become plutocratic. Thus, Sumner could argue that, whether democracy grew too weak or too strong, plutocracy lay in wait.[45]

To Sumner, perhaps the chief weakness of democracy resulted from the dogma of equality. Sumner did hold the egalitarian idea that each individual should be judged only for "merit and worth . . . without regard to birth, wealth, rank, or other adventitious circumstances"; but the notion that each individual should receive equal rewards was to Sumner obviously false and would establish base passions as the ruling motives in society. Dogmatic equalitarianism posited equal rights without equal duties which resulted in power for the democratic majority without corresponding responsibility and in duties for the responsible minority without corresponding rights. In this "unstable political equilibrium," Sumner argued, "dishonesty must follow"; and, as a result, plutocracy would necessarily emerge from the uninhibited workings of democracy.[46]

Sumner's awareness of human inequalities was mirrored in his ambivalence about the suffrage. How much his views, which originated in republican political theory, were affected by social Darwinism is unclear; but the combination of theories occasionally led Sumner to doubt the wisdom of a broad suffrage. To Sumner, the right of all men to vote on all subjects was less important than the community's right to good government. Thus, some men might be denied access to the political form so that the political essence could be preserved. In Sumner's view, the right to vote had to be balanced by the assumption of civic responsibilities. This view, coupled with his states'-rights position and his sympathy with white southerners, which stemmed from his elitism and his Louisiana experience in the contested election of 1876, led him to intimate in 1880 that at least temporary exclusion of southern Negroes from voting might be desirable. He was also led to argue that property owners could rightly claim a strong voice in municipal political affairs and that society's idlers should not vote. Sumner held that, while society might support the shiftless individual, it should never consent to be ruled by him.[47]

Despite Sumner's antidemocratic assertion that basic rights belonged to society and not to the individual, he did not always find the antagonism between the two irreconcilable. Thus, in 1877, he maintained the commonweal argument for good government; but he also made the Jeffersonian assertion that, "a wide suffrage is based on the experience that it conduces more to good government than a narrow one."[48] Similarly, he had stated a year earlier that political reform "does not seem to me to lie in restricting the suffrage or in other arbitrary measures of a revolutionary nature."[49] And in an undated fragment he wrote that, although opposed to democracy, "we do not deny [the] right of all men to share in the government, and if necessary, and at present equally."[50]

Clearly, Sumner had two broad objections to democracy. The first was that democracy would lead to social polarization, class war, socialism, and plutocracy. The second was that democracy stultified and leveled society downward. Instead of defending intellectual freedom, democracy followed mass opinion and promoted absolute orthodoxy—"big results on a pattern." For Sumner, the worst kind of society produced big results on a pattern.[51]

Paradoxically, Sumner also believed that, at its worst, democratic society possessed no principle of order because, in a sense, society and government mirrored the ruling masses whose "instinctive" lives were without conscious coherence, organization, or purpose.

Sumner's scorn for mass democracy underlines his unbending concern to discover the principle of social harmony through a science of society. Thus, he discovered in American history a movement from anarchistic liberty toward an ordered social system under law; and he regarded the Revolution, government under the Articles of Confederation, and the Civil War primarily as cases of temporary social disorganization.[52]

When Sumner wished to distinguish between a proper form of government and democracy, he recalled the Founding Fathers and their republic whose key words were "civil liberty" and "safeguards" and in which the people's function was periodically to confer power upon new agents. Sumner held that a constitutional republic should be strong enough for its limited purposes; therefore, like Hamilton, he supported federalism; and, like Jefferson, he advocated limited government. To Sumner, the best type of American statesman was a "Madisonian," "a moderate conservative man holding Jeffersonian dogmas and acting on Hamiltonian principles."[53] Republicanism demanded "high intelligence, great political sense, self-sacrificing activity, moderation, and self-control" from its citizens; but Sumner was not surprised that such "superhuman" demands had never been met, nor did he think they would be in the foreseeable future.[54]

In the foreseeable future, the facts of human nature required that republicans depend on the Constitution which was a concrete embodiment and guarantee of the principle of order. To Sumner, the Constitution's prime value was that it protected minorities against the "self-will" of majoritarian democracy. As previously discussed, Sumner had long believed that democracy was inevitable; and he had asserted in 1880 that "the men, the parties, the theories which oppose themselves to this tendency are swept down like seeds before a flood." Yet, he had immediately added, "there is a foundation for true constitutionalism in the traditions of our race and in our inherited institutions—in our inherited reverence for law."[55] Sumner believed that the "inestimable value" of the Supreme Court was that it had firmly protected civil liberty and lawful order and that it might prevent "pure" democracy. "If you take away the Constitution, what is American liberty and all the rest?" asked Sumner when he opposed the Spanish-American War; and he answered, "Nothing but a lot of phrases."[56]

Sumner's fervent constitutionalism revealed an inconsistency of which he sometimes became aware and which required him to

admit that the democracy which economic forces had produced
would inevitably override constitutional guarantees. Although democracy would then seem to rule unchallenged, Sumner hoped that
a free society would be saved by a virtuous elite. Behind constitutionalism stood Sumner's elite who would attempt to teach the
masses that liberty could be maintained only if "intelligent conscience and educated reason" were used to interpret written constitutions. Sumner's elite would teach that "constitutional institutions
of the best type fall into corruption and decay unless the virtues of
political self-control exist in high vigor and purity in the mores of
the society."[57] Sumner did not explain how the mores, which, like
democracy, were supposedly determined by economic forces, could
be either purified or maintained pure in opposition to both democracy and their own economic determiners; but he obviously believed
that individuals, even if they lived the instinctive life of the masses,
could choose or be taught to be virtuous.

A responsible teaching elite had to influence society through
political leadership; for, when it did not act, the vacuum was filled
by the scalawag, demagogue, and time-server.[58] Sumner spoke
consistently as a Mugwump when he called for good men to get into
politics; but his situation was complicated because he lived beyond
the Mugwump age into the turn-of-the-century era of imperialism,
monopolization, and Progressivism.

## VIII    *Normative Analysis of Democracy*

The foregoing discussion has shown that, despite his strictures
against it, Sumner viewed democracy as inevitable; but at times he
found democratic society not only inevitable but good. Sumner told
students in 1875 that democracy was represented by the worst
elements because the cultivated classes had been politically derelict:
"If they have culture, it is a duty, such as does not exist in Europe,
to make it work out from themselves into the life and activity of the
nation . . . so that the whole nation may improve together." "Of
course," he continued, "this is a great bore," compared to idling
under one's fig tree, writing a book, and not bothering about
politics. "But if this system of government is good for anything, the
only way in which it can do its work is . . . if a man has got anything
that would benefit other people, he is bound to make it available for
others."[59]

Sumner's criticism of democracy was generally so mordant that
his comparatively rare approving comments are easily overlooked.

But despite his social Darwinism, his conservatism, and his dogmatism, he was nevertheless so self-consciously American that he was deeply concerned about the fate of his country's experiment in self-government. Much of his criticism of democracy, therefore, was inspired by loyalty to it. For example, the spirit of his qualified approval of democracy appeared in an article of the mid-1890s where he indicated that "the whole genius" of America had inevitably been democratic. Furthermore: "No one will deny . . . that a democratic spirit has been breathed through all our institutions, has modified their action and determined their character. Opinions would differ as to whether its effect has always been good, but I doubt if anyone would deny that it has sometimes been good."[60] Sumner more often faintly praised democracy by loudly damning threats to his social norms as when he compared America to the image of decadent Europe. In 1870 he wrote that, although democracy deprived America of much that was good, he preferred to see the mass of people happy rather than burdened by a useless aristocracy as in England. And years later, while prophesying hopefully about America's future, he argued that Europe's problems were greater because of her "relics" of feudalism, kingly absolutism, and militarism.[61]

According to Sumner, imperialism was one of Europe's gravest ills, and his fear that American would soon sponsor imperial policy led him in his "Earth Hunger" essay of 1896 to recount the New World vision of the Fathers: "The fathers of this republic created a peculiar form of confederated state formed of democratic republics. They meant to secure us a chance to live in peace, happiness, and prosperity, free from the social burdens which had cursed the civilized nations of the Old World. We were to be free from war, feudalism, state church, balance of power, heavy taxation, and what Benjamin Franklin called the pest of glory."[62] That vision could be realized, Sumner continued, only in a land without subject peoples; for colonies would corrupt democracy. The old Federalists had known that a federation could succeed only when its members "were approximately on a level of political and industrial development."[63] Although Sumner often attacked theories of absolute equality, he believed that democracy could succeed only if political and economic conditions were relatively equal for all.

Sumner accepted a common nineteenth-century distinction between militarism and industrialism; and he believed that all societies faced an enduring conflict between the two but that industrialism represented the apogee of social evolution. Militarism referred to the cruder aspects of the past—war, imperialism, glory. Industrialism connoted the peaceful, happier characteristics of modern contract society. To Sumner, the means, ends, and mores of militaristic and industrial societies were irrevocably at odds. The antagonism between the two, he believed, "is the most important thread of philosophy which can be run through history."[64] Americans, Sumner warned at the turn of the century, must choose between two potential societies whose policies are typified by the questions "Will it increase our power to fight?" or "Will it increase the comfort of our people?"[65]

In Sumner's view, militaristic societies had been characterized historically by hierarchical, status, and privilege-oriented class structures; by monarchical, dynastic, absolutistic governments; by romantic, chivalric attitudes; and by submission to traditional authority and custom. War had been useful because it had taught men to value not only heroic virtues but also discipline, cooperation, fortitude, and patience. In Sumner's religious phase, war had appeared to him as part of God's disciplinary plan for men; but he consistently emphasized later that war had induced men to make broadly useful inventions. Like slavery, war had driven men toward civilization because it had destroyed outmoded institutions and had liberated "new social forces." Sumner found war difficult to categorize, however, for, like cannibalism or slave raids, it had both "societalized" and "dissocietalized." Sometimes war-induced social evolution had been terribly wasteful and had slowed the rise or the progress of civilization. On balance, Sumner opposed war; but he could not deny his belief that, at times, it had been socially useful.[66]

Sumner was similarly ambivalent about imperialism. Although he firmly believed that militarism and imperialism meant exploitation of colonies, an international arms race, and never-ending war, his Naturalism heightened his awareness of society's need to exploit nature wherever resources might be found in order to ease the struggle for existence. A consequent tension and ambivalence not only appeared in his discussion of national expansion but also ensured that his antiimperialism would be primarily concerned with the national interest. As in so many sensitive areas of his thought, Sumner was forced to differentiate closely and to narrow his definitions in his attempts to avoid paradox or contradiction.

Some of the tension in Sumner's thinking about national expansion was derived from his conflicting conclusions as to its probable causes and consequences. One of his reactions prior to 1898 and the Spanish-American War was to distinguish between political and economic expansion: "Political earth hunger," was merely "gratification of national vanity" but "economic earth hunger" grew from man's natural desire to live better. With this distinction, Sumner avoided a total condemnation of expansionism; and the same principle of efficient use of the earth's resources led him to support not only free migration of peoples and free trade but also economic expansion. Sumner viewed Britain as an approved example of enlightened and enlightening empire; for, instead of plundering outlying areas, it had planted new centers of civilization. Although Sumner admitted in 1896 that British colonization was to some degree political, he was not willing to equate it with vanity-ridden political earth hunger. The British method made earth hunger less "sordid" because it was an acceptable means "by which the human race occupies its patrimony, and by which civilization overcomes barbarism throughout the earth."[67]

When Sumner spoke of "the solidarity of the human race," he argued that all nations must advance together even if they did so on different levels. But, when he approvingly discussed expansionism, he was forced to distinguish clearly between civilization and barbarism and to present an embryonic conception of the white man's burden. Thus, with the gulf between civilized and noncivilized nations defined to Sumner's satisfaction, civilization was free to expand; indeed, it was required by humane motives to do so. The civilized were only assuming the patrimony that barbarians had neglected. Sumner's assumptions about economic expansion were consonant with biblical prescriptions to subdue the earth and with English philosopher John Locke's belief that "labour, in the beginning, gave a right of property."[68]

Thus, Sumner wrote in 1896 in "The Fallacy of Territorial Extension" that the slogan of "manifest destiny," which held that the United States must inevitably extend its hegemony widely, was partly true even though its ultimate rationale was power. Sumner also believed, however, that unthinking adherence to the slogan could create grave dilemmas for the United States, as in the case of Cuba; for, if that island fell into chaos, the civilized world might expect America to extend its jurisdiction. Sumner thought that, if America were compelled to govern Cuba, the task would be onerous and perhaps a "fatal calamity." The dilemma for Sumner was that, while the burdens of an expanding civilization were the "penalties of greatness," for America "All this will be disastrous to republican institutions and to democracy."[69] Sumner had clearly defined the dilemma by 1896, but the events of 1898 forced him to answer the question of whether or not the burdens of greatness would destroy America. Sumner answered by redefining the meaning of greatness.

Sumner's redefinition of national greatness took the form of a magnificent polemic against the Spanish-American War when, in one of the rare public addresses of his later years, he appeared in formal evening dress before Yale's Phi Beta Kappa society on January 16, 1899, and abruptly announced "The Conquest of the United States by Spain." His method was to juxtapose the Spanish symbols of militarism, imperialism, and absolutism and the American symbols of industrialism, peace, liberty, and democracy. His theme, and thus the irony of his title, was that the Spanish symbols had prevailed over the American ones.[70]

Above all, Sumner maintained, America symbolized self-government which included centrally the rational formation of public opinion on vital questions. That necessary democratic process, Sumner emphasized, had been grossly violated by those who had fomented the "Splendid Little War." The war had originated in domestic infighting by a little coterie of politicians; but, after the movement was under way, other interests had clambered aboard; and patriotic slogans had then stampeded the ignorant and honest. With public support enlisted, Sumner noted, opposition had been effectively silenced; for, after opinion had been established in a democracy, only the most virtuous—those with the greatest moral courage—dared dissent openly. False patriotism had enjoined silence "while our interests, our institutions, our most sacred traditions, and our best established maxims have been trampled underfoot."[71]

As always, Sumner was obliged to protest against injunctions to silence; and he scored the conservative classes of the country for dumbly acquiescing in the methods and dogmas that had been used to promote the war. Conservatives would live to regret their passivity, Sumner asserted as he paraphrased a sacred American maxim: The price of self-government, as of every other political good, was eternal vigilance. Americans could surrender this privilege, he warned, for Spanish pomp and glory; but, if they were devoted to governing themselves, why should they exchange that right for a glorious mess of imperial pottage? Sumner believed in 1899, as he wrote six years later in words which reflected his ministerial days and his sense of America's mission, that "This is not our calling as a nation."[72] Sumner also believed in 1899 that the apparent compulsion of Americans to abdicate self-government derived in part from ethnocentrism or "national vanity." Ethnocentrism revealed itself when the English, Germans, French, Russians, Spanish, Portuguese, Mohammedans, and Christians each regarded themselves as civilization's special agents: "The point is that each of them repudiates the standards of the others, and the outlying nations, which are to be civilized, hate all the standards of civilized men."[73] Imperialism violated the spirit of liberty both at home and in the case of the subject who was to be civilized.

Despite the cogency of his argument, Sumner was no more willing in 1899 than ever to relinquish the concepts of civilization and barbarism. Consequently, although he argued that the principle of liberty was universal, he was chiefly concerned with the effects of mixing a lower foreign stage of civilization with a higher American one. Sumner reiterated his consistent position that, as the Founding Fathers had known, member units in a political federation like the United States must be as homogeneous as possible, must be on the same stage of civilization and political evolution, and must have the same mores. The Civil War, he asserted, had occurred because excessive heterogeneity had developed in America.[74]

Despite Sumner's own ethnocentrism, it should not hastily be concluded that his utterances about liberty and related ideals were insincere. For example, when he referred to Spain's earlier decimation of Indian populations, he argued that the enduring cause of man's inhumanity to man was the belief that some men were not really men but that they were savages, heretics, and beasts. "Humane men and pious women" could be infected by this virus as were those Americans who regarded Negroes and Indians as lower orders that must be kept in perpetual tutelage. It is true that Sumner had never ardently advocated the principle of equality prior to 1899, except for the principle of equal opportunity. Indeed, his republicanism, social Darwinism, and anthropological-sociological investigations had convinced him that there was a wide natural range in human intelligence and ability. The crisis of the Spanish-American War, however, forced him to reveal clearly other equally deep-seated attitudes about equality. In 1899 Sumner opposed the conclusion that some men were incompetent to be free when he asserted the "relative truth" of "the doctrine that all men are equal." History, he declared, was the story of men crushing other men with the aid of the "beautiful doctrines" of religion, ethics, and politics. "Therefore, the doctrine that all men are equal has come to stand as one of the corner-stones of the temple of justice and truth. It was set up as a bar to just this notion that we are so much better than others that it is liberty for them to be governed by us." Americans, Sumner asserted, had held the doctrine of equality as an absolute despite the "glaring contradiction" that mention of Indians, Negroes, or Chinese revealed; but by 1899 absolute dogma had met Kanakas, Malays, and Tagals, and the dogma had quickly succumbed to Spanish doctrines.[75]

Put bluntly, in 1899 Sumner said about imperialism and equality what he had long held to be the golden rule of libertarian society: "Mind your own business." But Sumner's misfortune was that his belief in stages of civilization, his adherence to economic determinism, and his faith in the theories of Malthus all opposed that rule. Sumner's basic assumptions forced him to believe that the earth had to be claimed and developed by the most competent men and nations in civilization's perennial race against overpopulation. Thus, even in his antiimperialist argument of 1899, he admitted that territorial expansion was justifiable if a nation followed an enlightened economic program. The "Open Door" policy, which involved taking an area, policing it, and allowing free movement of commerce, was enlightened. All men were relatively equal, therefore, but those with enlightened trade policies were relatively more equal than others.

When Sumner returned to the political question in 1899, he reiterated his enduring position that American liberty, equality, and democracy had inevitably resulted from a protected situation in which America had enjoyed good land, few men, and no dangerous enemies. Since these happy conditions would inevitably disappear, Sumner maintained, as he shifted his argument from a descriptive to a normative tone, "Then liberty and democracy will cost something, if they are to be maintained." Imperialism would increase the cost and lead to the decline of democracy, for it meant "war, debt, taxation, diplomacy, a grand governmental system, pomp, glory, a big army and navy," and "political jobbery." Plutocracy, the "great foe of democracy," would certainly emerge from these unsavory developments because the chances for jobbery would multiply, popular interest in expansion would create a smokescreen for plutocrats, and public debts and taxes would increase. Higher taxes would make the poor poorer and the rich richer "because any social burdens bear more heavily on the weak than on the strong." Thus, Sumner concluded, "expansion and imperialism are a great onslaught on democracy."[76] Although Sumner advocated an equalitarian democracy in 1899, only a few years earlier in 1897 he had told students that all men were equal at zero—when dead—but at no other time.[77] The paradox is only apparent, however; for in the first instance he announced his unchanging social ideal while in the second he attacked, as usual, the straw man of absolute equality.

Sumner began the peroration of his 1899 speech with an argument that became common among formerly expansionist liberals whom the war had made antiimperialists.[78] America, a democratic republic, could not act as did a centralized monarchy without being transformed into an empire. "And yet," Sumner declared nostalgically, "this scheme of a republic which our fathers formed was a glorious dream which demands more than a word of respect and affection before it passes away." Actually, Sumner told his audience, it had been no dream at all but a reality to be grasped by those wise enough. Because America had been protected by geography, it had been able to take the best of European culture and to create a new civilization in the wilderness while it left inherited blunders behind. With virtually unlimited land, men had hoped that there would be no lordly classes, no pauper classes, and no idle classes. There would be no armies, no debts, no oppressive government, no imperialism; and "the vices of wealth would never flourish" in this "free democratic republic" where peace, industry, justice, and law would reign.[79] Now, these aspirations have not all been realized, Sumner admitted:

But it is by virtue of this conception of a commonwealth that the United States has stood for something unique and grand in the history of mankind and that its people have been happy. It is by virtue of these ideals that we have been isolated, isolated in a position which the other nations of the earth have observed in silent envy; and yet there are people who are boasting of their patriotism, because they say that we have taken our place now amongst the nations of the earth by virtue of this war. My patriotism is of the kind which is outraged by the notion that the United States never was a great nation until in a petty three months' campaign it knocked to pieces a poor, decrepit, bankrupt old state like Spain.[80]

When Sumner concluded, he bowed and left the stage. He did not leave the stage of American life for another decade, however; and during those years of the Progressive reform movement, the central question for Sumner, as for a wide range of Americans, was whether and how democracy could be preserved.

Over many years, Sumner's politically conservative views about democracy did not change fundamentally. What he called "pure" democracy had not been universally acceptable doctrine in his formative years nor was it entirely so in the late-ninteenth-century. Furthermore, Sumner characteristically drew upon earlier political theory; and, whether in a given instance it was Hamiltonian or Jeffersonian, it was conservative by later standards. His adventure into Naturalism served to justify his political conservatism and to intensify it in some degree. Nevertheless, in Sumner's thought a core of democratic belief stood against his complete acceptance of social Darwinism or a leap into authoritarianism. Sumner's ill fortune was, however, that his conservative political ideas and his desire to discover order and harmony in all things were challenged by the rapid changes of late-nineteenth-century America. Hence, his nostalgia and his fear developed as he faced an overwhelming future.

To a conservative political observer like Sumner, an obvious indicator of basic social change was the seizure of power by the masses. Every new step toward what came to be called "the welfare state" appeared as a fateful movement toward the abyss of social polarization and class war. Since constitutionalism and a sober elite appeared as flimsy defenses against a movement determined by vast economic forces, Sumner's political discussions mirrored a succession of apparent crises. He usually nagged at the heels of the democratic movement, but he discovered at times dangers worse than democracy, as when he attacked America's imperial outburst in the Spanish-American War. A major crisis in America's foreign relations was required, but it did call forth from Sumner a fundamentally democratic declaration that his ideal, self-governing, middle-class society could endure only if conditions of relative equality were maintained. It remains to be seen that a domestic crisis of similar magnitude in America's early-twentieth-century reform era elicited from Sumner an even more explicit announcement of the same belief.

## CHAPTER 7

# *Capitalism*

As a Naturalist, Sumner understood that all modern social institutions, including his ideal democracy, depended upon the fortunate economic circumstances of the age. If population outran food supply, if technological development slumped, or if men ceased to exercise the industrial virtues, civilization would decline, and democratic society would decay. Loyalty to middle-class democracy, as well as his Naturalistic outlook, led Sumner to focus his attention on society's economic foundation.

As preceding discussion has indicated, Sumner conceived that, since man's purpose was to live as well as possible under existing conditions, "self-aggrandizement" was "a law of life." Because, over millennia, instinct and intelligence had led men to "antagonistic cooperation" as the best method by which to achieve their purposes, mankind had advanced through the four stages of civilization: barbaric, hunting, pastoral, and agricultural. Although Sumner occasionally recognized that the stages were only convenient markers and that social evolution followed no determined order, he echoed his age and culture when he informed students that "the *Half-civilized* type is best represented in Southeastern Asia. The *civilized* is represented by our western civilization."[1] Over the four stages of civilization, he superimposed the more inclusive stages of militarism and industrialism. Sumner believed that, in the modern era, the most fruitful form of "antagonistic cooperation" had come to be industrialism, which was virtually his synonym for free-enterprise capitalism.

## I    *The Industrial Stage*

In 1900 Sumner warned that Americans must choose between militarism, which sought national power, and industrialism, which concerned itself with the people's comfort. He did not find the word "industrialism" entirely satisfactory, for "what we want is a term to

121

express the peace sentiment in antithesis to militancy"; but he thought the term did underline the necessity for cooperative production among all men in all stages of civilization. To Sumner, industrialism had developed from the struggle for existence, the competition of life, and the gradually perceived need among men for "antagonistic cooperation." Since cooperative organization had proved more efficient than individual effort, pooled resources had increased group power throughout history. Sumner believed that modern capital concentrations had contributed immeasurably to higher productivity and consequently had improved life conditions for all even if the capital had been managed by individuals who sought private gain. Ever-larger capital aggregations; the mutually beneficial expansion of free international trade; the great technological gains represented by the invention of gunpowder, steam locomotion, and electric communication; money; and the use of credit had all encouraged a more efficient centralized control over the industrial process. Finally, great modern discoveries such as that of the New World had offered vastly increased resources upon which men could exercise their organizational and productive ingenuity in their struggle to wrest a living from niggardly nature.[2]

A summary view of industrialism as it had evolved indicated to Sumner that economic and technological gains had given its devotees an increased power that had enabled them to take control of the state and thus to divorce industrialism from militarism. Sumner's sense of the efficacy of the private-profit motive led him to view the growth of modern industrialism as inevitable, and his general approval of its characteristics sometimes led him to interpret a tendency as an established fact. As he often indicated, however, industrial society retained numerous militaristic qualities and threatened continually to regress to a more primitive and militant stage. As previously indicated, Sumner's strong opposition to militarism was modified by his realization that from evil had sometimes come good and, similarly, that from good sometimes came evils or at least vices. To Sumner, materialism was perhaps the worst vice of industrial peoples, for it connoted love of luxury. But "mammonism," a word from Sumner's religious phase, was more exact because it expressed his unremitting scorn for a shallow worship of wealth. Another vice of industrial populations that Sumner noted was their tendency to softness and pusillanimity—their tendency to become industrial societies like China with a "vicious lack of military virtues and of patriotism." Sumner's list of industrialism's vices was, however, not extensive, for he attended primarily to its salutary characteristics.[3]

The economy, government, and society that Sumner identified with industrialism approximated the nineteenth-century liberal ideal. The economy was capitalistic, the government was republican or republican-democratic, and the society was imbued with capitalistic and republican virtues. Ideally, economic life followed the natural laws of production and trade so that private enterprise and private property were kept free from arbitrary governmental interferences. In a turn-of-the-century manuscript Sumner wrote in his defense of private property and in his antagonism to socialism that the "only land which can be communal is [the] graveyard."[4] The individual in Sumner's ideal industrial society was free to choose an occupation, to make contracts, and to compete with others so long as he recognized the necessity of cooperating with others in a sophisticated division of labor. Like the economy, government in industrial society was grounded on law; but, instead of being natural, governmental law was artificially enacted according to the provisions of a Constitution which guaranteed equal rights before the law and liberty that was limited only by the requirements of civil order. The industrial society that exemplified Sumner's ideals had a dominant middle class, monogamous marriage, popular as opposed to privileged education, and an emphasis on science and reason. Both its practical rewards and its mores encouraged the development of individual judgment, responsibility, and executive abilities; and its temper was peaceful, charitable, prudential, practical, "philistine," and prosaic.[5]

When Sumner wrote about international relations, his recognition of the value of extended "antagonistic cooperation" ensured his support of free trade, unlimited movement of populations, and peaceful international relations. This same recognition, which was also central to his domestic social views, helps to explain his advocacy of a harmonious society and his accompanying fears of class conflict and social polarization. Sumner believed that he advocated only what was natural when he wrote of harmonious industrial cooperation which was established by the laws of the universe and of human nature over which men had no control. He noted that, as Adam Smith had divined in discussing division of labor and as modern study showed, "antagonistic cooperation" between individuals and groups with "specialized differences" was natural; and he argued that the entire society, including perhaps

especially the weak, benefited from cooperation between its "superior and inferior" members; for "the struggles of the race as a whole
produce the possessions of the race as a whole."[6]

To indicate the naturalness of "antagonistic cooperation" in
society, Sumner often resorted to organic analogy as when, in *What
Social Classes Owe to Each Other,* he argued that modern capitalism
had freed men from other men and from nature because it had
encouraged organic division of labor and specialization: "The
modern industrial system is a great social co-operation. It is auto-
matic and instinctive in its operation. The adjustments of the organs
take place naturally. The parties are held together by impersonal
force—supply and demand."[7] As early as 1873 Sumner presented
the paradoxical image of a vast social organism whose members
were "endowed with free will to determine their own acts in
accordance with their own wishes."[8] Similarly, in 1888, he invited
the reader to consider all those who provided his food for a single
dinner: "All these thousands and millions of people, therefore, have
co-operated with each other for the common good of all, without
acquaintance or conventional agreement, and without any personal
interest in each other, under the play of forces which lie in human
nature and in the conditions of human existence on this earth."[9]
Sumner believed firmly that, whether men cooperated freely or
necessarily, nature's forces and laws pointed toward an organically
functioning industrial society.

## II    *Labor*

To Sumner, contemporary relations between labor and capital
illustrated that an organically functioning industrial society was
developing. In contracting to cooperate, both sides had antagonistic
as well as complementary interests "as is the case wherever supply
and demand operate." The worker's interest, of course, was to sell
his services as dearly as possible; but, in attempting to do so, he
could not legitimately ignore or override the natural law of supply
and demand because it offered the only valid measure by which the
worker's rewards could be established while social harmony and
maximum production were also maintained. The modern American
worker, Sumner believed, was rewarded very well indeed; for he
enjoyed unearned advantages that the discovery of a New World
and the inventions of a new machine culture offered. Historically,
Sumner taught consistently, fertile Western lands had provided an
avenue of escape for social failures and thus had kept demand and

wages high for the limited number of remaining workers so that no distinctly differentiated wage class had appeared. For those who stayed in settled areas, especially for those intelligent enough to sacrifice routine knowledge in order to adjust to new conditions, machines offered the freedom of a higher standard of living, greater physical and social mobility, and a more advanced civilization. Paradoxically, the machine had freed the masses of men from serfdom and slavery by requiring them to meet its sometimes coercive demands. When he admitted that the steam-age society was "machine-ridden," Sumner taught as always that freedom of whatever kind was not without its cost.[10]

Some workers, of course, were unwilling to pay the price of obedience to natural law and machinery; and they demanded not only higher wages but an eight-hour day. Sumner regarded such demands as arbitrary and as unfortunate because they ignored the laws of production and profit and because employers naturally responded unfavorably to malcontents. About the industrial war that resulted, Sumner was ambivalent; he sometimes found that it was natural and necessary, an inconvenient incident of liberty, or even a sign of vigor in free capitalism; for, by means of industrial war, employers and workers engaged in "antagonistic cooperation" to determine their share of the product. When he took this view, Sumner advocated laissez-faire as the best governmental policy regarding freedom of contract and competition in the industrial system. But, at other times, he found that industrial war was terribly wasteful and injurious especially to the consuming public which ultimately paid for the conflict through higher prices. Sumner believed that, if there was any reason to legislate against industrial war and thus to depart from laissez-faire policy, it would be to protect the public interest. When he concerned himself with the public interest, Sumner stressed that calamity waited for men who fought among themselves instead of against nature.[11]

Sumner was similarly ambivalent about labor unions and strikes because both were weapons in industrial warfare. He consistently criticized unions as monopolistic organizations that violated freedom of contract principles when they attempted to coerce government, employers, and laborers. He stressed particularly that energetic and ambitious workers were harmed because unions favored mediocre laborers by limiting apprenticeships and by "discouraging efficiency, conscientiousness, and excellence." Clearly, labor unions subverted the upward evolution of the race and of civilization.

"Idiots, insane persons, cripples, etc., are weak and society has to support them," Sumner argued in 1878. "Aside from these the strong are those who have the industrial virtues, and the weak those who have the industrial vices. Hereditary vigor and talent are the rewards of virtue in past generations. To shield the 'weak,' then, is to work the race downwards."[12] Sumner taught that "liberty of contract between adult men" was "the only proper principle in a free, self-governing state."[13]

To Sumner, history showed that strikes generally failed to withstand the economic forces of the law of supply and demand which set wages regardless of the wishes of employees. For workers to strike in an overcrowded industry instead of sensibly leaving it was "simply suicide." On occasion, however, Sumner virtually denied the validity of the English economist David Ricardo's "Iron Law of Wages" when he admitted that a well-organized and determined party could gain advantages in the industrial system because it possessed considerable elasticity. Sumner believed, therefore, that strikes served to test the market; for the law of supply and demand functioned only if participants in industrialism looked to their own interests. For labor to strike in order to discover if others would work for prevailing wages was sound political economy; but he warned labor that employers could exercise the same principle by locking out strikers and by hiring new workers at a lower rate. To Sumner, worker seizure of an employer's property and boycotts of an employer or his product were completely unacceptable strike weapons. Thus, although he admitted that strikes might be natural and useful, he so narrowly defined their legitimate scope and methods that had workers followed his wishes they would have found strikes of little use.[14]

Sumner's view of unions was much like his view of strikes. Although he viewed unions as monopolistic and as debilitating, he also admitted that they were potentially valuable to workers and to the industrial system. Unions could offer members useful information about the labor market and about industrial conditions, "maintain *esprit de corps*," and cultivate their public image; but they could legitimately do little more, even in the present. As for the future, Sumner wrote in 1883 that "the development of individualism is to be looked forward to and hoped for as a great gain. In the mean time the labor market, in which wages are fixed, cannot reach fair adjustments unless the interest of the laborers is fairly defended, and that cannot, perhaps, yet be done without associations of laborers."[15] Although Sumner was probably less sanguine in his later years that his hopes would be realized, he continued to wish for the day when the independent laborer could freely contract with his employer without coercive intermediaries; but his essay of 1888 on "Trusts and Trades-Unions" concluded that the union was "a monopolistic organization on the side of labor entirely parallel with the trusts on the side of capital. . . . The nineteenth-century trades-union is a nineteenth-century institution, as much or more so than the ring, pool, corner, or trust. They are all products of the same facts in the industrial development, and one is just as inevitable, and, in that sense, legitimate, as the other."[16] Legitimate or not, Sumner was worried about the coercive power of both trusts and unions. Some commentators, he continued in 1888, denounced trusts but suggested that the cooperation and combination of capital and labor could solve the labor question. Contrarily, Sumner warned that the combination "would be the most gigantic 'trust' that could possibly be conceived."[17] Sumner was troubled by the dangers of monopolies whether they were spawned by labor or by capital; but the mere suggestion of a combined monopoly of the two stirred his deepest fears for middle-class society.

Rather than a monopoly of capital and labor, Sumner preferred law-abiding unions and peaceful strikes. Labor violence was, of course, reprehensible to Sumner; and he argued that it would not only endanger society but would harm laboring men. Sumner occasionally explained, as a student noted and misspelled early in the 1880s, that "Carl Marks' " theory of a proletarian revolution took inadequate account of capital's ability to buy talented leadership, arms, and even a proletarian army to battle an insurrection of the poor. Furthermore, violence against capital would encourage it to become plutocratic.[18]

Although Sumner grudgingly admitted the limited value of labor organizations in industrial war, he spoke most strongly for a peacefully cooperative and organically functioning industrial society that could best reward all of its members. His appeal to the natural laws of supply and demand and of "antagonistic cooperation" combined the authority of classical economics and evolutionary science. The findings of both taught him that workers—and the weak and inferior generally—should endure present trials because the natural evolution of capitalism would bring rewards far greater than would a revolt against the industrial discipline. The working-man who read Sumner learned that both the harsh conditions caused by overpopulation and the good times created by industrialism coerced the individual; and he also read that, in either case, the individual gained whatever freedom man could enjoy through cooperative enterprise.

### III    *Capital and Capitalists*

Sumner's discussions of the labor question reveal his tendency to alternate between recitations of the abstract tenets of classical economics and attempts to analyze actual capital-labor relations. The same ambivalence appeared when he examined the rising power of capital and capitalists; for, with a Naturalist's concern for material foundations, he praised the "captains of industry" who organized and directed business enterprises. The frequency and the tone of his comments suggest that he considered them to be members of his elite, but his praise was reserved more for their utility than for their disinterested public service. Sumner believed that the medieval era had elevated warriors and priests but that the nineteenth century's dominant concern with economic development had produced a new "psycho-physical" type that was represented by steelmaster Andrew Carnegie—a type that had replaced the landed nobility as *the* power in society. From Sumner's viewpoint, natural selection had produced the captains of industry because of their natural monopoly of the "rare and indispensable" gift of executive talent. Consequently, since no man could make his million dollars without helping the millions, it behooved the lower ranks to pay cheerfully the price exacted by industrial generals and to bear with those who were "masterful, arrogant, and overbearing," even when they lived in vulgar luxury. More alarming to Sumner than their arrogance was the probability that such masterful leaders would recreate monopoly in their own interest, but he tended to assume that the natural cycle of combination and competition would maintain industrial equilibrium.[19]

Sumner's doubtful attitude toward the *nouveau riche* sometimes turned sarcastic, as when he wrote of an unnamed meat baron in an aside that was deleted when his manuscript was published posthumously: "A little while ago an ignorant boor, a pig-butcher, worth a million or two, having learned my occupation, said to me: 'I don't see no use in no colleges. My boy don't want to go to college and I'm glad of it. I tell him that I've got on a great deal better than any of the eddicated fine gentlemen I know and I never had no eddication at all.' "[20] Sumner admitted, no doubt sadly, that the pig-butcher was not entirely wrong.

Sumner's vision of society's elite as composed of highly responsible individuals who disinterestedly pursued the common good helps put his attitude toward the captain of industry into proper perspective. While the elitist worked through persuasion, the master of industry coerced society. Sumner assumed that self-interest was the captain's basic motivation; and, to Sumner, as an advocate of Adam Smith's argument that the combined self-interest of individuals somehow equaled the social interest (an argument that Naturalism seemed only to update), the captain's self-interest appeared to be both natural and right. As a hard-headed realist—that is, as a classical economist and as a Naturalist—Sumner believed that the present state of human nature precluded any other rationale than self-interest for motivation; and yet, his elitist ideal belied his assertions that captains of industry could not be expected to make disinterested sacrifices.

Whether or not Sumner recognized the contradictions in his beliefs about human nature and motivation that a comparison of the elite and captains of industry reveals, he was never completely satisfied with industrial leaders who benefited society from consequence rather than from purpose. As Sumner turned from religion to Naturalism, he began to insist that, in the real world, consequences only and not purposes had to be considered. Thus, in Naturalistic terms, captains of industry might be a new elite; but, since Sumner was not always able to respond as a Naturalist, purpose continued to affect his judgment. Thus, doubly armed with his Naturalistic ethic of effectiveness and with elements of his earlier moralistic business ethic, he could attack both those who demanded that the state chastise the slightly tainted but highly effective captain of industry and those who sought wealth from the state rather than through their own labors. How Sumner varied the use of his ethical systems may be clarified in discussions of plutocracy, monopoly, and the regulation of business.[21]

## IV   *Plutocracy*

Although Sumner shared the widespread late-nineteenth-century fear of plutocracy, his responses to the danger were inconsistent. As a minister, he defined and attacked plutocracy in 1870 as "the very worst form of human society which the world has ever seen."[22] A few years later, he identified plutocracy broadly with "the new aristocracy of wealth . . . with its mercantile code, and its counting house standards" which engaged in "the most flagrant worship of the golden calf."[23] But his acceptance of Naturalism forced Sumner to narrow his definition of plutocracy from a generalized term for the power of crass materialists and to use the term only for those who gained wealth through *political* rather than through economic means. The captain of industry, therefore, need not be a plutocrat; and plutocracy did not inevitably follow industrial development.[24]

Sumner was required to distinguish clearly between plutocrat and capitalist because of his Naturalistic vision of the value of industrial organizers and of the vital function of capital in the advancement of civilization. The logic of his position sometimes led him to deny the social power of capital and almost to deny that of plutocracy. In 1878 he asserted that there were "no class privileges and no special protection to wealth" in the United States. A few years later, in 1884, he rejected as false the popular belief that business, particularly corporate enterprise, was then more oppressive than formerly. Mere accumulation of wealth, he asserted in 1894, did not equal plutocracy because wealth had to be defined by its use. To prove that plutocracy existed, Sumner argued, it had to be demonstrated "that great wealth is, as a rule . . . put to a mischievous use"; but, to him, the power of money was then almost exclusively industrial and only slightly political.[25]

Despite such near-denials, Sumner always considered that plutocracy was a fundamental threat to his ideal society; and he tried to explain why it appeared in American democracy. One of his methods was to argue that, when the demos, or the masses, sought absolute Socialist equality, it violated the principle of republican political theory that private property interests could legitimately claim influence in government. The demos attacked private property when it legislated unearned gains for itself, passed confiscatory legislation, or refused to pass laws necessary for industrial development. Sumner never tired of warning that, when legitimate power was denied open recognition by whatever method, such power was driven underground to become warped plutocracy. Although Sumner tended to blame the demos for creating conditions that invited plutocracy, he occasionally noted, especially when he discussed the protective tariff, that the money power also initiated dangerous social struggles. As a lifelong free-trader, he viewed the tariff and other instances of "jobbery" as attempts by powerful political and business interests to seize control of the state, to buy votes, to create privileged classes, and thus to subvert democratic society.

Sumner's fear that plutocracy would prevail intensified in the 1890s and even more in the new century's era of business concentration and reform ferment. In 1898 he wrote privately, "I am . . . of the opinion that the money loss by corporations is a lesser evil than political corruption of all our institutions by the Tammany system with big spoils, jobs, offices, etc., etc., but it is a direful choice." [26] In 1905 he stated publicly that America was no longer a democracy, for it was ruled by "oligarchies. The captains of industry . . . do not mind this, for it gives them something which they can deal with better." [27] In an article of the following year, Sumner reiterated the theme that "lawmakers can sell their power to make laws, and masters of industry can buy what is for their interest." [28] During that same year, in a free-trade speech, he also asserted that the government was conducted by "a combination of . . . protected interests"; but he then noted that "there has been within the last year or two a very great revolt in the public mind against graft and political and business corruption. How far will this go? We do not know, but it is . . . an opening in the public mind that is full of chances. It may go very far; it may have very great effects; it is certainly something to be noticed and taken advantage of." [29] By 1909 Sumner had decided that the incompetence and the Populism of the Democratic party was paralleled by "the more and more complete surrender . . . of the Republican party to the character of a conspiracy to hold power and use it for plutocratic ends." [30]

Sumner attacked plutocracy somewhat less than demos because of his allegiance to the benefits of organized power. But he certainly hated the implications of plutocracy as much as those of mobocracy; and he just as certainly was not primarily concerned with its causes. Sumner could blame either the masses or the capitalists or the interaction of both for causing plutocracy because his ultimate loyalty was to the middle class. Sumner's loyalties to a class, as well as to Naturalism, help explain the contradictions in his views of monopoly and the regulation of business.

## V  *Monopoly*

Contradictions in Sumner's attitudes toward the problem of monopoly are reflected in the varying definitions that he applied to the term. He identified three broad types of monopoly—natural, artificial, and what might be called "mixed"—and all of these ranged in degree from absolute to imperfect. Sumner's conception of natural monopoly was relatively straightforward and consistent; for he meant that nature's supplies were limited, that the use of a natural agent thus excluded others from its enjoyment, and that natural monopolies were never social creations but were "facts in the order of the universe." A partial list of such monopolies included transportation routes, communication lines, utilities, capital, paper currency, talent, physical force, beauty, learning, and, of course, virtue. Although these and other natural monopolies were ineradicable, Sumner noted that men had gradually learned to control the genii of power in natural monopolies as when they used beasts of burden, fire, wind, water, steam, or electricity. Men had harnessed natural forces in their struggle from savagery to civilization, a stage that benefited all men. But, inevitably, the immediate possessor of a natural monopoly benefited more from it than the average man—a situation which merely illustrated the fact of universal natural and social inequality. Sumner admitted, however, that state regulation of natural monopolies such as railroad lines was possibly desirable.[31]

When Sumner discussed artificial monopoly, he fell into a morass of shifting definitions. As Sumner turned from supernaturalism to Naturalism, he shifted from a broad definition of artificial monopoly to a narrowly political connotation as he had also done in the case of plutocracy. In 1879 he had defined monopoly as "interference with supply and demand by individuals, combinations, and governments"; but this all-inclusive definition proved troublesome precisely because opposition to all interferences with the market directly opposed Sumner's later recognition of the value of combined capital in industrial development. His reaction was to identify "artificial monopoly" more with legislatively created combinations and less with private combinations.[32]

The "popular rage," he argued in 1883, should not be directed against private combination but against legislative jobbery. Sumner's opposition to state-created artificial monopolies was unremitting, for he believed that "state and market" should be separated to avoid a ruinous evolution toward socialism and plutocracy.[33] Sumner distinguished between legislatively and privately created combinations because he subtly transmuted the latter into "natural" phenomena—which required that he give the word "natural" a double meaning. The first meaning related to his definition of natural monopolies; the second meaning applied to the natural evolution of industrialism. According to the second meaning of "natural," he was able to regard giant private combinations and quasi-monopolies, which had earlier qualified as artificial monopolies, as "natural" developments. Thus, government should both forbear meddling with the natural industrial growth of private combinations and eliminate all artificial legislatively spawned monopolies such as those created by tariffs.

The natural development of industrialism, as Sumner construed it, was only a special case of the universal evolutionary process by which all things moved toward realization of their own potential along an alternating or oscillating course which involved assimilating and repelling, or combination and competition. As he wrote in *Folkways,* "competition and combination are two forms of life association which alternate through the whole organic and superorganic domains."[34] From this alternation, civilization had arisen; but, in the present stage of industrial evolution, Sumner believed in 1902, combination prevailed. This swing of the universal movement—the concentration of wealth—was "but one feature of a grand step in societal evolution" that included unions as well as trusts.[35]

Sumner repeated a common nineteenth-century conservative argument that, since trusts were both inevitable and good, to tamper with them was unwise. For worried citizens, he offered the consolation that the natural dialectic of the universal movement ensured that monopoly and competition were "continually interlaced—merely different phases." New inventions and changes in production methods tended to bring disaster to monopolies and to revive competition; and, as monopolies mushroomed, their "internal cohesion" inclined to weaken and crumble. Furthermore, a monopolist could never arbitrarily establish price because of his inability to control demand. Finally, Sumner distinguished between bad ("narrow") and good ("broad") trusts. In their attempts to hold production down and prices up, the narrow trusts instigated economic, political, and international wars. This narrow policy had characterized earlier European mercantilism, and Sumner feared a twentieth-century revival of it. Conversely, he preferred a broad trust policy of large volume production and sales with small profit per item, and he hoped that it would prevail because it was economical.[36]

Monopoly, Sumner argued, would fade into competition, and competition would in turn fade into monopoly; for a cosmic process—one that men need not and could not control—directed industrial evolution.

## VI   *Regulation of Business*

A radically different aspect of Sumner's concern with industrialization related to possible government regulation of it. Sumner was not opposed to all state control of business, but his support for it was relatively weak and infrequent. Fear of plutocracy had led him to express concern about corporate growth early in his career when he testified before a congressional committee in 1878 that "I am rather inclined to the opinion that we have got to have a struggle with the great corporations before we get through, but I have not any programme for it." Despite the disclaimer, he continued, "I think we have not yet learned to charter corporations and still exercise the necessary control over them in the public interest."[37] Unlike his later emphasis on the natural evolution of industrialism, Sumner believed in 1878 that the great corporations should somehow be regulated because the public interest was opposed to huge, unregulated aggregations of wealth. Even in *What Social Classes Owe to Each Other* of 1883, which is usually taken as a classic laissez-faire argument, Sumner showed concern about the new industrial power when he called for better regulation of the stock market and for new constitutional guarantees against plutocrats—the "new foes"—in order "to hold the power of wealth to that responsibility without which no power whatever is consistent with liberty."[38]

Sumner invariably opposed the regulation of business through such agencies as the Interstate Commerce Commission because he believed they attempted to fuse administration and jurisprudence and were subject to social whims. Instead of this "German" practice of granting bureaucracies the power to interpret and enforce laws, Sumner preferred the "Anglo-American system" which worked through law, left interpretation to the courts, and left the individual free and responsible. Sumner apparently never considered that law and the courts could be subject to social whims. But even as Sumner opposed the Interstate Commerce Commission, he admitted that railroads had to be regulated to some degree.[39]

A distinction between the "ideal" and the "real" must be recognized in Sumner's thought. Ideally, Sumner believed, laissez-faire would be practiced. Despite the ideal, however, he realized that "laissez-faire is a maxim of policy. It is not a rule of science."[40] As Sumner believed, the businessman hoped that the legislator would "'let him alone' and, if possible, not legislate about his affairs at all."[41] But Sumner accepted, even if reluctantly, the view that regulation became increasingly necessary as society grew in numbers and in complexity. His realization that the ideal was not at least immediately realizable deepened Sumner's pessimism about American prospects, for regulation created the explosive combination of politics and economics: "The reason why my political pessimism offsets my economic optimism is that I cannot see how, under existing conditions, industry can be set free from political control, and I do not see how economics and politics can be reconciled so that industry can prosper and law can be respected, both at the same time."[42] In this statement of 1905 Sumner faced an unpleasant reality that he had not been inclined to see in writing about the "Separation of State and Market" in 1889. When realism demanded his admission that the growth of trusts had caused abuses that had to be corrected, Sumner wrote at the turn of the century that trusts would require the proper regulation that the joint-stock companies had and that proper "devices" would gradually be developed.[43]

Sumner's vagueness about proper devices of control indicated clearly that he was not primarily concerned with the regulation of business. He remarked in 1902 concerning the tremendous growth of corporations like United States Steel that "it is not my duty in this place to make a judicial statement of the good and ill of the facts I mention—I leave to others to suggest the limitations and safeguards which are required. It is enough to say here that of course all power is liable to abuse."[44] While Sumner did not reject business regulation, he revealed his practical conservatism in that he left the details of regulation to others while he viewed industrial growth as a natural process in which government could offer little help and much harm; and, as always, he used the logically opposed images of the overpowering inevitability of the industrialization process and the delicacy of the industrial system. The inevitability of the process indicated the futility of political intervention, and the delicacy of the system warned against rash experimentation.[45]

Since rash experimentation was the social scientist's particular bugbear, Sumner's conservatism and dedication to careful scientific investigation characteristically buttressed each other. Consequently, his discussions of business regulation stressed that both practical experience and scientific knowledge must precede legislative action. Because, to Sumner, the worst kind of rash experimentation was based on "ethical" preconceptions, he attacked President Theodore Roosevelt in 1907 as a principal offender in the current financial panic because he had made "indiscreet denunciations" of business leaders generally, whereas only a few were culpable. Moreover, Roosevelt had stirred "far worse evils" when he had disrupted business and had frightened investors: "What we have seen is but the beginning of what is to be expected—confusion and wrangling, with stagnation of industry, suppression of enterprise, and a loss of the great and joyous energy which has hitherto characterized our people."[46] The loss of energy, joyous or otherwise, was a painful prospect for Sumner to contemplate; and, even though he admitted that the regulation of business would be necessary, he continued to wish that such controls could be avoided so that the people would be free to devote their energies to the industrial development that advanced civilization.

The logic of Naturalistic assumptions led Sumner to accept the growth of huge industrial enterprises and to accept wholeheartedly the industrial discipline. Like other Naturalists, he believed that men must inevitably be coerced into submission to the industrial process as they sought power over nature in the struggle for existence. In the drive for power, "secondary considerations" had to be brushed aside; for consequences flowed from efficient causes, not from ethical or philosophical purposes. Those who sought a material base upon which to build the higher aspects of civilization had necessarily to accept certain discomforts such as a degree of arrogance from industrial generals, a lag in the development of legal regulations, and the slow, uncontrollable alternation of combination and competition. Sumner's attempt to allay his own as well as the public's fear of monopoly depended upon the assumption that monopolization was only one-half of the natural alternation of combination and competition.[47]

In retrospect, this assumption appears to have supported a most damaging faith in such alternation—a faith which was paralleled only by Sumner's effort to persuade unfortunate sufferers in the industrialization process to rely upon the healing function of a cosmic cycle. When he discussed the combined competition and combination that "antagonistic cooperation" represented, Sumner assumed that the individual would protect himself even when he pursued interests that were not purely individual in their nature. But, in Sumner's larger theoretical conception of the alternation of competition and combination, he left the individual virtually at the mercy of impersonal process. Critics of Sumner's social Darwinistic emphasis on struggle have tended to view it correctly as conservative, as class oriented, and as opposed to the interests of the weak, the downtrodden, the workers.

But it should be recognized that Sumner's abiding concern with the social peace, harmony, and equilibrium which he expected natural law to establish had much the same effect because it led him to stress that class consciousness and social conflict were as counter-productive for the oppressed as for oppressors. Committed as he was to natural law prescriptions, Sumner linked social evolution to the Industrial Revolution—an act which, for all his conservative opposition to reformist meddling, was most radical. Sumner's participation in the modern drive to define change, particularly technological change, in terms of social improvement belied at times his conscious conservatism; and, when he viewed industrialization as natural, inevitable, and good, Sumner ignored his otherwise generally consistent dictum that power, like knowledge, had the potential of being either for good or for evil.

## VII   *Reform*

As the preceding chapters about Naturalism and about democracy have suggested, Sumner's mature thought contained two parallel and potentially opposed strains. One, normally dominant, stemmed from an intellectual acceptance of Darwinian Naturalism with the result that the strong economic emphasis in Naturalism encouraged Sumner to defend the growth of large American industries; for big business would produce the most. In addition, Sumner's application of the Darwinian hypothesis to the social structure led not only to his expectation of a wide and socially beneficial range between individuals and classes but also to his strictures against advocates of absolute equality.

The second strain in Sumner's thought did not normally find clear, overt expression. Indeed, since it was based less upon reason than upon emotional commitment, it seems often to have been suppressed and to have appeared only in crises like the Spanish-American War. The reference, of course, is to the strong and pervasive ideal in the early-twentieth-century Progressive era of a middle-class capitalistic and democratic society. Sumner's ideal found its clearest expression in an essay of 1909 which he and later editors of his work never published.[48] This typescript essay, "On the Concentration of Wealth," was a plea that the good society be restored. America, Sumner asserted, was threatened by monopolies; and, like many of his contemporaries, he now demanded in the name of democracy that conditions which offered equality of opportunity be restored. He warned that, if they were not, if great inequalities of wealth continued to inhibit opportunities for open competition, social war would result. Loyalty to the state and to society, Sumner argued as he cited Daniel Webster and Edmund Burke, grew neither from political theory nor from abstract philosophy but because the interests of individuals were satisfied.[49] Sumner wrote that, as Webster had truly realized, even a politically free government would soon fall if its laws allowed wealth to concentrate in a few hands while the majority remained "dependent and penniless." Sumner's perennial fear of social polarization and class war permeated the essay.

Sumner asserted in 1909, as he had come to believe in the early twentieth century, that internal war threatened and that, although society was ruled formally by representative assemblies, it was actually ruled by a "small controlling oligarchy" of monopolies because the laws had permitted monopolization. In terms that were similar to Muckraker Ray Stannard Baker's comments a few years earlier about the formation of United States Steel, or of Progressive Woodrow Wilson, a few years later, Sumner declared that "already huge accumulations of property by corporate consolidations, accumulations such as the world has never before seen, are subject to a single control. A single corporation determines the destinies of more human beings than the King of Denmark or the Queen of Holland."[50] Sumner wrote in "On the Concentration of Wealth" that to seek anew the causes of monopolization was urgent, "for in an exposure of causes lies the only hope for discovery of remedies." In this essay, sociologist Sumner became indistinguishable from Sumner the polemicist; for, like the Progressive Muckrakers, Sumner always aimed to "expose" the underlying causes so that responsible citizens could discover remedies; but the causes that required exposure were now considerably different from those of an earlier day.[51]

The ultimate cause of present conditions, Sumner asserted in 1909, was simply that "size secures monopoly." Sumner now abandoned the qualifications and extenuating arguments of his earlier writings and drove to what he conceived to be the heart of the matter: to his conviction that the nature of power led to its use and that, in business as elsewhere, the law of "self-advancement" was as natural as that of self-preservation. It must be realized, Sumner insisted, that ever-larger capital formations were created to multiply power and that "the faculty of size is to overbid, to undersell, to extrude competitors."[52] To Sumner, the methods by which size secured monopoly were manifold: a trust could virtually control the market; an overwhelmingly wealthy trust could purchase threatening competitors; and, if they refused to sell, the trust could overbid and undersell until the opposition was crushed. The purchaser's "simple precautions" would then bar new competitors, and the trust could extend both horizontally and vertically: "Industrial strength then adds to itself consequential civil and political powers, and the combination is monopoly in its recognized form." It was also, of course, a fearful plutocracy.

The consumer is in the forefront of this 1909 essay. Normally, Sumner's first concern as a Naturalist had been with production, investment, and industrial growth although he had wavered occasionally in favor of the consumer. But, in 1909, he supported the Progressive emphasis on the public interest.[53] When monopoly existed, he wrote, the public soon realized that "monopoly and duress" were synonymous because one bought from the monopoly or not at all—and did so on the monopoly's terms: "The public's alternative is the definition of monopoly." "The 'cost of living,' instead of being an expression of the needs and resources of society adjusting themselves through multitudinous transactions in a resultant, is fixed by central authorities; they limit the output and control the prices of crackers, hams, sugar, salt, kerosene, chewing gum, matches, glue, soil and sewer pipe, radiators, sewing machines, etc. Competition with them offers little hope of success; existence at the terms of their indulgence is not the full measure of social freedom."[54] The natural laws of supply and demand that Sumner once had relied upon no longer seemed to function. Although he had once argued that political meddling had caused imperfections in the market, he had come to believe that laws had been too permissive because the "central authorities" of government had been replaced by the directors of monopolies. Sumner could make no fine distinctions among the types of monopolies that existed because he admitted that a monopoly by any name represented coercion.

To Sumner, the prime example of the socially effective man had earlier been the captain of industry, even though he had sometimes been critical of the captain; but in this 1909 essay the captain was not even mentioned—perhaps because he was morally implicated but most certainly because he had been the instrument of a disastrous monopolization process. Earlier, Sumner had criticized the inept and meddling "politician"; but now he appealed to the disinterested and responsible "statesman." The statesman's duty, Sumner quoted Edmund Burke, was to discern the "latent wisdom" in public opinion; and presently, he must recognize the legitimacy of growing demands that "real and practical" equality of opportunity be restored, which could only be done by limiting the size of corporations. Sumner naturally repudiated socialism's equality of property and reward, and he did not want corporations destroyed since modern civilization demanded them. Significantly, however, this consistent theme in Sumner's earlier thought was muted in the 1909 essay "On the Concentration of Wealth." Sumner had earlier envisioned that alternating combination and competition would raise men through the stages of civilization, but the theory that competition would resume when sufficiently large units had developed was absent in the 1909 essay. Sumner could therefore no longer make a distinction between "broad" and "narrow" trusts; and, in an apparent reference to Rooseveltian doctrine, he asserted that attempts to distinguish between good and bad trusts were pernicious.

As a minister and as a Naturalist, Sumner had considered industrial issues in individualistic and moralistic terms; but in 1909 he no longer praised or censured individuals. According to his former standards, the bad individuals—the plutocrats—were winning; and the good individuals—the "Forgotten Men" who always practiced the industrial virtues—were losing. To Sumner, it would have been a strange world, indeed, in which honesty, saving, and hard work were rewarded with disaster while those who practiced immoral methods triumphed. Since Sumner refused to accept such a nightmare, he was forced both to condemn the product of industrial evolution and to call upon the state for succor. By at least 1909, since Sumner had come to believe that the nature and logic of the system and not individuals had produced the evil, industrialism was no longer an absolute good to him but a relative good that had to be carefully controlled to prevent social catastrophe. In changing his attitude toward industrialization, Sumner had not abandoned moral judgments late in his life; he had only shifted his criterion so that it was now neither the religious nor the narrowly Naturalistic standard of survival value. Rather, his criterion was now in a broad sense democratic because he desired to protect relative economic and political equality in a middle-class society. The true end of democratic government, he believed in 1909, was that "each may have equal opportunities of life, liberty, and the pursuit of happiness." In desperation, Sumner drew upon phrases from the Declaration of Independence, the same phrases which earlier had appeared to his conservative constitutionalism as mystical products of Jefferson's natural rights theory.

Sumner had taught in his earlier years that law must not infringe upon the individual's freedom to engage in business combination, but he invoked the protection of the state and of democratic symbols in 1909 to defend the larger freedom of all to compete on relatively equal terms. Wrestlers, he wrote, grapple according to weight; but this practice is impossible in the marketplace, for no law or court can force equality of competition between unequals. Sumner had always argued that liberty and equality were antithetical, and he had written in 1905 that "there is no reason at all to expect that economic development will ever come into harmony with the political ideals of liberty and equality."[55] But, convinced in 1909 that plutocracy was crushing the middle class, Sumner believed both that ideals were not separable into economic and political spheres and that no liberty could exist without equality.

Clearly, Sumner did not wish to revolutionize but to conserve America's social, political, and economic life. He was thus impelled late in his life to defend middle-class ideals and at least temporarily to disregard Naturalism; for his middle-class democracy, even if capitalistic, was considerably different from the society predicated by Naturalistic logic. As Sumner now recognized, "the rivalry of unequals is destruction."

## VIII   *The State*

When Sumner came to believe that America's middle-class society faced destruction, he called upon the state, or government, to restore the ideal. To seek governmental assistance was anathema to a laissez-faire theorist and to a Naturalist like Sumner who had always attacked Socialists and plutocrats for such behavior, but his ultimate emotional commitment caused surprising changes in his tactics. Furthermore, although he may have made what seemed only an expedient compromise, his action revealed a fundamental inconsistency in his view of the state. To Naturalist Sumner, the state as it actually functioned was only an instrument of force; and the popular belief that government existed to provide justice was untrue. History showed that the state was not a sovereign entity and that societies always had a ruling class which seized power for its own purposes. Democratic self-government only worsened matters, as American history with its demos, plutocrats, and politicians revealed, because all interests in a free society were free to scramble for the prize.[56]

When he discussed the state, Sumner tried to speak as an

impartial scientist of society and as a realist, but he also occasionally allowed himself to consider how things ought to be. As nineteenth-century liberals believed, and as Sumner had learned in college, the government's ideal mission was to guarantee peace, order, property, liberty, right instead of might—which meant equality before the law—and justice. Sumner believed that government should stand as an impartial arbiter above all individual, interest-group, and class interests in defense of the public interest. Thus, while he rarely spoke for regulation of business, he always did so in the name of the public interest. When Sumner discussed the ideal state, he was a nostalgic Utopian of the golden past, as when he wrote in 1880 of John Quincy Adams's administration that "it presented no heroics whatever, neither achievements nor scandals, and approached, therefore, that millennial form of society in which time passes in peace and prosperity without anything to show that there is either government or history."[57] In 1887 he compared contemporary "socialistic" tendencies to the American past in which "the state has existed of itself."[58] Two years later, he expressed his perennial hope that "Separation of State and Market" could be achieved if only the government practiced self-denial, although he could find no evidence that any ruling class had ever done so. Yet, if democracy offered "any great hope for mankind," it was that the state would break the common mold and return to the precepts of Jeffersonian democracy; for, Sumner wrote, "it was not afraid to be called nongovernment or 'atomistic.'"[59] Somewhat like Karl Marx, Sumner looked forward to the day when the state, if it had not withered away, would have at least shriveled to its former size.

From one of Sumner's perspectives, government was a weapon in the social struggle; from another, it presided over society as an impartial judge. In the first instance, government was only "all-of-us" who were trying to seize the weapon. In the second, it was reified; as ideal, it became an entity with its own life as an impartial arbiter in an ideal laissez-faire society. Sumner never managed to reconcile the real and the ideal because his understanding of human nature would not permit him to take a sanguine view of government as it actually functioned, and his laissez-faire idealism would not permit him to relinquish the impartial arbiter state.[60]

Perhaps Sumner's greatest illusion was to believe that he acted disinterestedly in the ideal world of the public interest when he was actually an interested partisan in the real world. The sources of his illusion were intensely personal not only because they were derived from his self-image as an expert, impartial, scientific member of society's elite but because they also depended upon his middle-class ideals and loyalties. In Sumner's view, the strategic position of the peacemaking middle class between the warring proletariat and the plutocracy and this class's inestimable value as the one "from whom alone any important contributions can be drawn" made it indispensable to the public welfare. As previously discussed, both Sumner's ideal middle class and his ideal elite were psychologically nonclasses that either minded their own business or served society selflessly. Sumner's view of the elite and the middle class as noninterested groups, combined with his view of the state as impartial arbiter, allowed him to identify personal interests and loyalties with the commonweal and ultimately to call on the government to protect and defend the public interest by preserving a middle-class, capitalistic democracy. In doing so, Sumner responded much like a middle-class Progressive.

Progressivism, as Ralph Henry Gabriel has recognized, and as other investigators have substantiated, was composed of a heterogeneous and often conflicting "potpourri" of groups and interests which were drawn from virtually all socio-economic classes and which sought to control their own destinies by reforming a rapidly industrializing society. Numerous Progressives were in the middle range socially and economically; but, like individuals from other groups, the middle-class Progressives were not necessarily in agreement about either their fears and hopes or their means and ends. Significantly, however, many of them felt a conservative and nostalgic urge to defend a relatively equalitarian, capitalistic, democratic system—what Sumner considered a middle-class society—by somehow controlling the growth of plutocratic big business monopolies in order to restore equality of opportunity. Because Sumner had felt this central urge for several years, he was like numerous other nineteenth-century liberals who began around the turn of the century to support Progressive reforms; but not until 1909 did Sumner openly call upon his ideal state—his normative "democracy"—to rescue "the people" from the "trusts."[61]

Not surprisingly, Sumner's appeal was both late and vague because he was old, tired, and conservative. Throughout his career, Sumner had expended much intellectual energy in defense of the nineteenth-century liberal's vision of freedom. He had occasionally recognized that freedom had to be regulated somehow, but he had left details to others while he had pursued the antithetical enterprise of working to separate state and market. Sumner's 1909 essay "On the Concentration of Wealth" shows clearly, however, that, before either program was formally enunciated, he rejected the principles of Theodore Roosevelt's New Nationalism, which proposed generally that big government regulate big business; and he accepted the principles of Woodrow Wilson's New Freedom, which, at least as campaign rhetoric, abhorred leviathan monopolies and appealed to a nostalgic conception of free, equal, and open competition among business units of manageable size. Consequently, it seems probable that Sumner continued to hope that state and market could be separated and thus frustrate plutocracy, the current major enemy of middle-class democracy. Then industrialism could continue its evolution while government would have the only slightly enlarged function of ensuring that economic combination did not again grow beyond bounds.[62]

During the nineteenth century, a major American assumption was that equality of opportunity actually existed; and it followed, at least for laissez-faire liberals, that the government's duty was only to preserve an independently existing condition and that its positive role was unnecessary and potentially dangerous. Sumner once wrote that the duty of government was simply to protect the sanctity of property and the honor of women.[63] But, especially with the rise of industrialism and a more complex commercial society, groups which had never enjoyed the full measure of opportunity, or which felt that opportunities were decreasing, began to protest increasingly. In the Progressive era, the middle-class groups joined the widening circle of protesters; and all disaffected parties inevitably turned to the government for redress. For, whether government was viewed as an impartial arbiter or as an instrument of class power, it was assumed to be the one effective social agency that could control rampant industrialization.

As a proponent of laissez-faire Naturalism, Sumner had defended middle-class society and democracy through his attacks on either plutocracy or mobocracy or both. To fill the vacuum created by his taboo against appeals to the state, he had appealed as a Naturalist to the social evolution that occurred according to self-equilibrating natural laws. But, after his confidence in benevolent natural evolution had been shaken, Sumner had little to offer except the nineteenth-century liberal's emphasis on individual morality and self-restraint. Little was changed in principle when he appealed in 1909 for the moral and impartial arbiter, the government, to end industrial monopolization. But the enormous implications of Sumner's shift in tactics, combined with those of a great many other individuals and groups of the Progressive era, would be revealed in the expanding role, status, and power of American government in the twentieth century.

## CHAPTER 8

# *Conclusion*

WILLIAM Graham Sumner was eminently successful as a professional and as a public man. As an educator, he saw his reform ideas begin to prevail; and he won remarkable popularity and respect for his teaching. As a polemicist dedicated to the education of the masses in the scientific laws and in the facts of economics and sociology, he was widely published and read. For more than thirty years the press regularly sought his comments about public matters. He published respectable works in economics, political science, and history. Although obituaries in 1910 remembered Sumner as a teacher and economist, his later reputation came gradually to rest primarily on his pioneering work in the science of society. *Folkways* was a major work that immediately earned and has continued to hold the respect of sociologists.

### I   *Forgotten Man*

Despite his varied accomplishments, Sumner is remembered by few today. In the eight years following his death, the Yale University Press published four volumes of Sumner's essays, many of which had not previously appeared in print. Harris E. Starr, an Albert Galloway Keller student, presented a biography in 1925 published by Sumner's friend Henry Holt. Since 1925, Sumner has been little noticed except in histories of sociology and as a social Darwinist. A few scholars have presented excellent discussions of Sumner's Naturalistic viewpoint and laissez-faire individualism, but no one has published a balanced appraisal of Sumner's thought and writings.[1]

The possible reasons for such stress on Sumner's social Darwinism and such inattention to other aspects of his thought and writing are various. A minor reason is that Sumner's manuscripts, some of them richer and more varied than his published essays, were uncatalogued

146

for many years and were mixed indiscriminately with those of Albert Galloway Keller. Another reason is that, as a publicist, he addressed current issues; and many of those issues have seemed irrelevant to a later age. A more important reason concerns Sumner's harsh, dogmatic tone and style which cause his most striking phrases to be of a social Darwinistic or deterministic nature while his discussions of "antagonistic cooperation" and harmony are less obvious and sensational. Furthermore, because of personal proclivity and ideological position, Sumner was an academic independent who was out of touch and sympathy with most other major American pioneers of sociology.

In addition, he did not create a strong school of sociology at Yale University; and, despite the efforts of Albert Galloway Keller, sociologists have considerably limited their studies of Sumner's ideas. Moreover, Sumner's reputation as a sociologist has been limited because he did not live to complete and publish his "Science of Society." When, nearly two decades after Sumner's death, Keller completed the work, his rigorous attempt to preserve Sumner's ideas resulted in an outmoded emphasis upon the unilinear evolution of societies through stages of civilization which found little favor with sociologists and anthropologists who had begun to stress a relativistic cultural pluralism.

Evidence, much of it in rough unpublished manuscripts intended for inclusion in the "Science of Society," indicates that Sumner's cultural outlook was broadening in his later years. Wide-ranging studies in a dozen languages of the customs and mores of many and varied peoples had somewhat modified Sumner's moral absolutism and his cultural ethnocentrism. As a dedicated young disciple, Keller tried honestly to fulfill the vision and outline of his mentor, but he inevitably lacked Sumner's deeper understanding. With all the honesty of purpose at his command, Keller could not write another man's book and fulfill an older, more sophisticated man's vision. Furthermore, Sumner's "Science of Society" notes and manuscripts were inadequately prepared for Keller's purposes. Thus, although they often expressed in their clearest, most complete, and most carefully qualified form the ideas that were only adumbrated in Sumner's lectures and essays, they were not published. More than once Sumner wrote poignantly that "the greatest ill on earth is that the older men get the more they know what to do and how to do it and the less able they are to do anything. All else is trivial compared with that. It is the reason why all progress is so slow. The knowledge and power, and the will and the power are not united. [The] young are strong and through ignorance waste strength. [The] old are wise and through age are powerless."[2]

Finally, as Sumner's editor, Keller's understanding of the meaning of his thought, especially as it related to science, helped to shape the view of Sumner that has prevailed. Keller selected essays for publication with an eye to the image of Sumner as a scientist who was centrally concerned with empirical, cold, hard facts. And, while Keller was not entirely incorrect, he published little of the modest amount of Sumner's manuscript material which was imaginative, speculative, and philosophical and which revealed Sumner's belief that without hypotheses, as well as facts, there could be no dialectic of science and no human progress. Keller was, however, only minimally responsible for Sumner's obscurity; for the most important cause was the nature of Sumner's own personality and character as he expressed them in his writings.

## II    *Quest for Harmony*

Sumner was born in 1840 in a society which was, despite intimations of future developments, still essentially agricultural and commercial in orientation and which had a vast frontier, few railroads, and no imperial standing in the world. Before the Civil War was over, and late in the Western age of absolutes, Sumner had been indoctrinated in the faiths of Protestant Christianity, classical economics, and republican democracy. When he died only four years before World War I burst upon Europe and America and at the virtual height of the Progressive era, he was the citizen of a major world power that was being revolutionized in its social and intellectual life by industrialization, urbanization, a million immigrants annually, and the unending ramifications of Darwinism.

In his mature years, therefore, Sumner was forced to reconcile old assumptions, ideas, and faiths with new conditions and world views. In light of his personality and training, the moderate success he achieved in his reconciliation of old and new is impressive. Some indefinable combination of heredity and environment influenced young Sumner to become a moralistic perfectionist who was ambitious yet upright, disciplined and duty bound, and an advocate of the conservative Golden Mean. His training—especially in his father's work ethic, in religion, and in political economy—formed in his mind a series of absolute truths and images about the ideal nature of man and society; but he had also learned that change and growth were essential to both man and society and that the scientific method could discover truths. Thus, Sumner met Darwinism not with uncompromising resistance but with a predisposition to find the truth in it.

When, as Sumner wrote in a revealing phrase, he was "definitely converted" to evolution, he accepted the new faith with all the rigor of a convert. His attitude seemed to be that, if change and evolution had to sweep away the absolutes of the moment, he would discover that flux was the absolute essence of the universe; and he would devote himself to the study of social evolution—by means of an amoral scientific method—with characteristic moral fervor. He would by force of will consciously eliminate the emotional, romantic, unreasoning urges; and he would become the complete and rational scientist. By so doing, he would join the scientific, rational, scholarly, and prophetic elite leadership of the era.

Sumner once told Keller that he had had two waste periods in his life, one as a preacher and the other as a politician. No doubt they seemed wasteful to Sumner for both different and similar reasons: his religious period had been wasted, Sumner came to believe, because he had preached antiquated superstition; his political period had been wasted because he had not cared to learn and spend his energies practicing the rules of the game; and both periods had been lost time to Sumner because they had required skill in the arts of compromise and ambiguity. On the contrary, Sumner was best equipped temperamentally to serve as an expert who spoke with authority that was based on absolute laws and truths that men had only to obey in order to achieve personal and social harmony. Both early and late, the pattern of Sumner's life and writings reveals that he sought the comforting certainty of universal law whether it was expressed in religious terms or in the doctrines of political economy and the new sociology. Sumner's ideal self-image was that of the Realistic and Naturalistic scientist who had managed to eliminate Romanticism, Idealism, Utopianism, and Subjectivism from consideration.

Obviously the insidious danger of an elitist image of the objective scientist was that it would be believed and that the scientist's quest for the absolute certitude of law would mask his faith with a scientific facade. The danger was that the scientist would come to identify himself with infallibility and would ultimately fall victim to the ancient sin of *hubris*. Sumner believed that he had suppressed Romanticism; but, when he wrote about the great forces of human nature, such as man's atavistic tendencies or the sexual force expressed in Malthusianism; when he employed images of suffering and death in man's struggle for existence against the pitiless forces of nature; or when he imagined the crushing, uncontrollable force of great cosmic cycles, his Romanticism was as authentic as that of literary Naturalists like Frank Norris or Jack London.

Similarly, the concepts of evolution, oscillation, harmony, and "science" generally, although purportedly objective and scientific, at times served Sumner's subjective interests and loyalties although he probably was not capable of conscious hypocrisy. Although the ultimate implications of evolutionary theory militated against a conservative or status quo position, evolutionism could also serve to emphasize that natural social changes must be glacially slow and free of artificial private and public meddling. And, insofar as Sumner used evolutionism to support his social Darwinism, it served to validate capitalistic struggles.

Like evolutionism, Sumner's conception of dialectical oscillation was conservative because it ensured that change would be tethered to some midpoint to which it must inevitably return. Sumner's Naturalistic studies convinced him of the reality of man's struggle for existence and the competition of life; but they also taught him of "antagonistic cooperation" which provided a mechanism that harnessed struggle in the interests of cooperation, peace, progress, and harmony. Oscillation enabled Sumner to reconcile the struggle he saw in the real world with the ideal of harmony because both struggle and harmony obeyed natural law. But, not incidentally, the concept also encouraged Sumner to assure factory workers, reformers, and worried citizens that industrial monopolization and any incidental warping of the democratic process was only a temporary phenomenon. Harmony, likewise, implied balance between extremes, which was Sumner's Golden Mean and which was, at its first appearance, an unexceptionable ideal. But the labor organizer or reformer who read Sumner's essays surely recognized his middle-class myopia and asked at whose expense social harmony was to be realized.

Sumner, a man of great forcefulness, was paradoxically aware as a Naturalist that men were puny creatures in a great arena where overwhelming forces in clashing interaction created the "conjunctures" in which men must live. Although he believed in his early mature years that man and Providence cooperated to build the Kingdom of God on earth, and although he believed always that human intelligence and exertion had brought men upward in the stages of civilization, he nevertheless gradually abandoned or lost his grip on the Enlightenment faith that a benevolent force in the universe worked for man. A late exception to Sumner's growing pessimism was his argument, which he ultimately relinquished, that the growth of business combinations expressed that benevolent force. Sumner concluded in time, and perhaps with a certain grim fascination, that man was subject to atavism, social decay, and the inconceivably vast gas-to-gas cycle of cosmic flux; that he was left alone in the universe to direct his own destiny to the limited extent possible; and that, where he could not do so, he had to find meaning in his existence by seeking to understand the natural forces and laws that directed him.

Sumner's sense of lonely man in an alien universe also extended to his vision of an American society that was alive with monolithic forces—especially plutocracy and proletariat—which were indifferent to any fate but their own and whose struggles shaped the social conjuncture in which the "Forgotten Man" of the middle class was threatened with extinction. Clearly, the wearing fear that imperialism and industrial monopolization would destroy the "Forgotten Man's" freedom to seek self-realization led Sumner at times to reassert the democratic faith. He had absorbed that faith in earlier years and had never been able entirely to deny it despite the attractions of elitism and Naturalism. How deeply Sumner believed in the shield he finally seized to defend his ideal of relatively equalitarian democracy is less certain. Since fear for democracy's continued existence could scarcely have dissipated Sumner's lifelong distrust of the government, it appears that only desperation could have forced the appeal.

In his later years, like other disillusioned Naturalists and prophets of cataclysm, Sumner increasingly opposed with mingled nostalgia and despair the sweeping popular optimism of his age and country. Not long before he died, Sumner told his friend Keller that he had lived through America's best years and that he would prefer not to live into a twentieth century filled with social conflicts and wars.[3] Sumner's tentative and unstable faith in the ability of man and in that of his institutions to shape a decent democratic future had been much weakened over long years by his competing faith in Naturalistic determinism. Yet, the force of the older faith had exerted itself even in 1909, and Sumner had called upon his fellow citizens to follow the path of reform instead of resignation.

### III    *Summary*

This study of Sumner's thought and writings over a long and productive lifetime in an age of social and intellectual revolution has necessarily focused on weaknesses, inconsistencies, and unfortunate consequences of his ideas and beliefs at least as much as upon his successes. But, to evaluate Sumner's contribution as a writer and scholar, it is necessary at last to reject his own dictum that consequences alone and not purposes must be considered; for, when one weighs the value of a man's life and works, there surely can be no adequate judgment of consequences without consideration of his purposes.

Sumner intended always to seek the truth and to see things whole and clear, even in a world in which respectable evidence taught him that truths were no longer absolute and enduring. Thenceforth, as he pursued elusive, changing truths, he was sustained by the faith that order and harmony prevailed—or could prevail—in the universe. Sumner believed that men could perceive universal order by using self-correcting scientific methods and that men could then use the laws of nature to ameliorate the human condition.

Man's condition could best be improved, or at least be made bearable, if men cooperated to protect individual freedom and opportunity. If Sumner were to be remembered only as a libertarian champion of the freedom of the mind, of critical and disciplined thought, and of academic freedom, he would be well remembered. As an American educator and public man, he taught consistently that individual freedom and opportunity could best advance both the individual's and society's interest in individual self-realization and could thereby best preserve a democratic republic. Self-realization, as Sumner used it, was a Naturalistic conception; but its origins, which he did not normally acknowledge, were in the older democratic assertion of the individual's right of equal opportunity to education, property, liberty, and the pursuit of happiness. In economic matters, Sumner's concern for self-realization and the public interest led to his demand that citizens and governments follow a laissez-faire policy that supported freedom of contract and enterprise at home and free movement of trade and peoples across ethnocentric barriers internationally.

In Sumner's view, individual and social freedom would promote peace and harmony in American society and throughout the world. As a Naturalist, sociologist, and defender of capitalism, Sumner reminded men that they must work and cooperate in peace so as to live as well as possible. As an elitist and as a partisan of the middle class, he spoke for the commonwealth and for a just, relatively equalitarian society governed not by conflicting factional and class interests but by law. As a man of peace in international relations, he attacked militarism and the Spanish-American War with all the facts and argumentative and rhetorical skill at his command. Cooperation and peace, Sumner fervently believed and taught, were at least as natural and necessary as struggle and war.

Throughout his life, Sumner's purpose was to serve and to lead in the attempt to create better men and a better society. His ambition was not merely for wealth or reputation; he desired to serve society and his fellow men to the limits of his ability. To Sumner, service was no humble occupation but a duty that *noblesse oblige* required. Thus, service and leadership were ultimately inseparable. As a publicist, public servant, teacher, and scholar, Sumner always attempted to educate the people in democracy by calling attention to pressing issues and by offering reasoned argument based on scholarship rather than on demagogic rhetoric. His arguments and evidence were sometimes narrow and, as his critics believed, dogmatic and biased. His harsh rhetoric not only exacerbated at times the social conflict that he sought to end but also helped prevent the social harmony for which he yearned. But Sumner assumed that the dynamics of learning depended on conflict between viewpoints and that his duty was neither to defend every possible position nor to tread softly upon opponents.

The duty of the publicist and scholar in democracy was to require the people to think and especially to think about matters unpleasant and sacred. The alienating effect of Sumner's elitist and Naturalistic views enabled him to question central assumptions and faiths of his era even as he shared to some degree in a sense of their sacredness. Hence, perhaps, the iconoclast's thoroughness in smashing idols— the dogmas of natural rights and of the infallibility of democratic majorities; the smug belief in inevitable and unending material and moral progress; ethnocentric self-deification in a nation and era that could glorify the Spanish-American War and make a hero of Teddy Roosevelt.

The qualities that impelled Sumner to serve as iconoclast and prophet also made him an intellectual pioneer. Despite his considerable rigidity and dogmatism, which were partly the products of his training in absolute truths, and despite his conservative fear of drastic and unpredictable change, Sumner was able to change his mind. He could relinquish a long-argued and well-developed position, as he did in 1909, or even a world view that seemed at odds with facts and reality, as he did in the 1870s.

Sumner's intellectual influence was significant and extensive in his own era. His defense of laissez-faire policies undoubtedly helped impede the acceptance of the Welfare State; but Sumner passed from the scene, and the Welfare State eventually prevailed. Sumner influenced the discussion of the tariff, currency, and taxation issues; but those issues, in their nineteenth-century form, are dead. For a third of a century Sumner helped shape the social philosophy of many Yale students who became and remained influential in America's economic and political life far into the twentieth century; but Sumner's students, too, have passed from the public scene. Sumner and others of his era laid the foundations of American sociology—for which later sociologists have expressed proper appreciation; but those sociologists inevitably turned to building walls on the foundations or, perhaps more accurately, interior partitions; and they did not think much about the foundations. When, however, *Folkways* was most recently reprinted, in 1979, the publishers remarked that the book was "among the few enduring monuments of American sociological theory" and that Sumner's concepts of folkways, of in-groups and out-groups, and of ethnocentrism continued to inform much contemporary sociological thought.

Whether Sumner's ideas will in the future be of more than historical interest depends partly upon whether Americans seek whatever significance the past may have for their present. Whether Sumner's ideas retain any importance also depends upon whether, as Americans face perennial issues in new guises, they look to past thought for specific prescriptions or for attitudes of mind. It is certainly true, as Sumner reiterated tirelessly in his central teachings, that people in society must continue in their attempts to balance and to control power relationships—between the individual and society, among the multitudinous economic and other interest groups in society, among the nations in international society, and between people and machines. But Sumner had few or no specific and practical prescriptions that could be used to cure social ills a century or more later. If his thought offered such panaceas, history would hardly be a process of constant flux.

In evaluating the thought and influence of William Graham Sumner, this book must end as it began—by judging that Sumner's enduring significance derives less from specific acts and ideas than from qualities of mind and character that he intended always to bring to bear upon the perennial problems of man in society. As a man and scholar, Sumner possessed the moral courage and concern to peer into mysteries in which there were no eternal verities. Despite waverings induced by personal ambition, Naturalistic relativism, and the mesmerism of his own rhetoric, Sumner tried to live by an ethical system. That system elevated the moral absolutes of honesty, work, responsibility, and moral courage. Some may judge that Sumner was hypocritical when he publicized ideals to which he did not completely adhere; or they may conclude that he was merely weak and inconsistent; but they should ask what such a man would have been with no ideals and no moral code.

As Sumner's life and writings reveal, moral absolutism has its dangers; but so, as observers of the morally jaded late twentieth century may admit, has the moral anarchy that Sumner warned against in the last pages of his great last book, *Folkways*. In an age of unimaginable excesses that are calmly rationalized, Americans may well remember William Graham Sumner's plain speaking in the name of moderation.

# Notes and References

## Chapter One

1. Note from [Clarence Day] to Albert Galloway Keller, n.d. Manuscripts are in Yale Historical Manuscripts and Archives unless otherwise indicated.

2. Except where otherwise noted, biographical information is taken from the following: Harris E. Starr, *William Graham Sumner* (New York: Henry Holt, 1925); Register of Walton le Dale, 1821, County Records Office, Preston, England; "Sketch of William Graham Sumner," *The Challenge of Facts and Other Essays*, ed. Albert Galloway Keller (New Haven: Yale University Press, 1914), pp. 3–13; William Graham Sumner, "Autobiographical Sketch of William Graham Sumner," *Earth-Hunger and Other Essays*, ed. Albert Galloway Keller (New Haven: Yale University Press, 1913), pp. 3–5; Albert Galloway Keller, *Reminiscences of William Graham Sumner* (New Haven: Yale University Press, 1933); letters from Sumner to Jeannie Elliott, 1870.

3. *Challenge of Facts*, p. 3.

4. Starr, p. 56.

5. Letters from Sumner to Jeannie Elliott, May 2, 1870; Apr. 30, 1870.

6. *Challenge of Facts*, p. 5.

7. George Wilson Pierson, *Yale College: An Educational History, 1871–1921* (New Haven: Yale University Press, 1952), p. 9.

8. Starr, pp. 34–35. See also Laurence R. Veysey, *The Emergence of the American University* (Chicago: University of Chicago Press, 1965), pp. 22–23, 26–27, 36; Jurgen Herbst, *The German Historical School in American Scholarship: A Study in the Transfer of Culture* (Ithaca, N.Y.: Cornell University Press, 1965), pp. 26–29.

9. Starr, p. 32.

10. Ibid., p. 20.

11. Letter from Sumner to Jeannie Elliott, Aug. 9, 1870.

12. Letter from Keller to Clarence Day, June 1909.

13. Veysey, p. 440; Stow Persons, *The Decline of American Gentility* (New York: Columbia University Press, 1973), p. 183.

14. May 26, 1874, William C. Whitney Correspondence, Historical Manuscripts Division, Library of Congress.

15. Starr, p. 53.

16. Ibid., p. 61.

17. *Challenge of Facts*, p. 6.

18. Starr, p. 66.

19. *Challenge of Facts*, p. 7. See also Herbst, pp. 14–20, 53–57.

20. Letter from Sumner to Jeannie Elliott, Aug. 12, 1870.

21. Keller, *Reminiscences*, p. 97.

22. Jan. 20, 1873.

23. "Individuality and Societality," [c. 1900], n.p.

24. Letter from Sumner to Jeannie Elliott, May 4, 1870.

25. Ibid., May 2, 1870; June 20, 1870; Sept. 27, 1870.

26. Ibid., July 7, 1870.

27. Ibid., June 16, 1870.

28. Ibid., June 6, 1870.

29. Ibid., Sept. 23, 1870.

30. Ibid., Oct. 9, 1870.

31. Ibid., May 19, 1870.

32. Ibid., Sept. 20, 1870.

### Chapter Two

1. Note in file drawer 18, n.d. Notes are housed in Sumner's original file.

2. *Folkways: A Study of the Sociological Importance of Usages, Manners, Customs, Mores, and Morals* (1906; rpt. New York: Dover, 1959), p. 637.

3. Ibid., pp. 6–7; William Graham Sumner, *War and Other Essays*, ed. Albert Galloway Keller (New Haven: Yale University Press, 1911), p. 135; *Earth-Hunger*, p. 18; Lectures on "Science of Society," transcribed by A. L. Bishop, 1902–1903, semester 2, lecture 31; Lectures on "Anthropology," transcribed by Keller, 1896, n.p.; Lectures on "Science of Society," transcribed by Keller, May 28, 1896.

4. Lectures on "Systematic Sociology," transcribed by Keller, May 11, 1899, p. 24.

5. Notes in file drawers 3 and 14, n.d.; *Earth-Hunger*, p. 255; Lectures on "Social Science," transcribed by Keller, Feb. 24, 1897, n.p.; "Progress," [c 1900], n.p.; "Sin," [c. 1902], p. 41; *War*, pp. 24–25.

6. Lectures on "Mental Outfit," transcribed by Keller, May 17, 1899; Starr, p. 24.

7. Starr, p. 25.

8. European Journal, pp. 1–3; Sumner had courted Hattie Morgan for a time when he was in college.

9. Starr, p. 63.

10. Ibid., p. 65.

11. Letter from Sumner to Dr. Elias Beadle, June 10, 1866.

12. *Challenge of Facts*, pp. 8–9. See also Herbst, pp. 7–8.

13. Starr, p. 102.

14. Letter from Sumner to Jeannie Elliott, May 22, 1870.

15. "Review of the Month," *Living Church*, Nov. 1869, p. 99.

16. Sermon no. 26, July 12, 1870; "The Solidarity of the Human Race," 1873, n.p.; "The Living Church," *Living Church*, May 1869, p. 4; "Review of the Month," *Living Church*, Apr. 1870, p. 177.

17. Notes in file drawers 9 and 19, n.d.

18. *What Social Classes Owe to Each Other* (New York: Harper, 1883), pp. 158–59.

19. "Review of the Month," *Living Church*, May 1869, p. 1; "Notes," *Living Church*, July 1869, p. 42; "Review of the Month," *Living Church*, Dec. 1869, p. 114.

20. "Book Notices," *Living Church*, Aug. 1869, p. 59.

21. "Notes," ibid., p. 57.

22. "Review of the Month," ibid., Feb. 1870, p. 147.

23. Ibid., Mar. 1870, pp. 162–63.

24. Ibid., June 1869, p. 17.

25. Starr, p. 119.

26. Ibid., p. 120.

27. Ibid., pp. 155–56.

28. Sermon no. 116, Nov. 11, 1871; Sermon no. 146, May 24, 1872.

29. Letter from Sumner to Jeannie Elliott, May 16, 1870.

30. Sermon no. 104, Sept. 16, 1871.

31. Sermon no. 78, May 11, 1871.

32. Sermon no. 105, Sept. 22, 1871.

33. Sermon no. 17, July 16, 1869.

34. Sermon no. 146, May 24, 1872; *Challenge of Facts*, pp. 354–55; "Review of the Month," *Living Church*, Mar. 1870, p. 161; "The Public School Question," *Living Church*, Jan. 1870, pp. 133–35.

35. "Review of the Month," *Living Church*, Jan. 1870, p. 131. See also "The Solidarity of the Human Race," 1873, n.p.

36. Letter from Sumner to Jeannie Elliott, Aug. 6, 1870.

37. Untitled [college class note], n.d., n.p.; "T [heodore] Dwight's Lecture on Christian Evidences and Natural Theology," n.d., n.p.

38. Sermon no. 17, July 16, 1869. See also Sermon no. 80, May 28, 1871; D. F. White, "Summons for the Kingdom of God on Earth: The Early Social-Gospel Novel," *South Atlantic Quarterly*, Summer 1968, pp. 469–85; Ernest Lee Tuveson, *Redeemer Nation: The Idea of America's Millennial Role* (Chicago: University of Chicago Press, 1968), pp. 1–90 and passim.

39. Letter from Sumner to Jeannie Elliott, Aug. 4, 1870.

40. Letter from Sumner to Jeannie Elliott, Apr. 30, 1870. See also letter from Sumner to Jeannie Elliott, June 14, 1870.

41. Sermon no. 82, June 3, 1871.

42. "The Living Church," *Living Church*, May 1869, p. 3.

43. Letter from Sumner to Jeannie Elliott, June 10, 1870.

44. Sermon "Farewell Discourse," Sept. 6, 1872. See also Sermon no. 148, June 7, 1872; Sermon no. 33, Aug. 25, 1870.

45. Letter to C. W. Squires, May 20, 1874.

46. Sermon no. 46, Oct. 28, 1870.

47. "The Church's Law of the Interpretation of the Scriptures," 1872, n.p.

48. Sermon no. 115, Nov. 7, 1871.

49. Sermon no. 2, June 20, 1868.

50. "Introductory Essay," 1872, pp. 22–23.

51. "The Living Church," *Living Church*, May 1869, p. 3. See also "Review of the Month," *Living Church*, June 1869, p. 17; Sermon no. 16, July 16, 1869; Sermon no. 148, June 7, 1872.

52. "Introductory Essay," 1872, pp. 13–14.

53. Sermon no. 10, June 12, 1868.

54. Sermon, "Farewell Discourse," Sept. 6, 1872.

55. Sermon no. 14, June 17, 1869.

56. Letter from Sumner to Jeannie Elliott, Sun. eve., n.d.

57. Keller, *Reminiscences*, p. 43; Starr, pp. 542–43.

58. Starr, p. 543.

## Chapter Three

1. Letter from Sumner to Jeannie Elliott, Apr. 30, 1870.

2. Letter from Jeannie Elliott to Sumner, Sept. 22, 1870.

3. Letters from Sumner to Jeannie Elliott, June 6 and 12, 1870.

4. Letter from Sumner to Jeannie Elliott, July 7, 1870. See also letter from Sumner to Jeannie Eliott, July 8, 1870.

5. Letter from Jeannie Eliott to Sumner, July 6, 1870.

6. Ibid., July 16, 1870.

7. Letters from Sumner to Jeannie Elliott, June 6, July 11, and Aug. 19, 1870; Letter from Jeannie Elliott to Sumner, July 6, 1870.

8. Letter from Sumner to Jeannie Elliott, June 6, 1870. See also Starr, pp. 79, 123.

9. July 5, 1872.

10. Letter to Lord Archibald Campbell, May 29, 1874.

11. Herbst, pp. 19–20, 29–30, 49.

12. "The 'Ways and Means' for our Colleges," *Nation*, Sept. 8, 1870, pp. 152–54.

13. Nov. 1869, p. 98.

14. Letter to Keller, [c. 1905]. See also "To the Meeting of Professors in the Academical Department," n.d., n.p.; Starr, pp. 335–42.

15. *Living Church*, Jan. 1870, pp. 133–34. See also "Review of the Month," *Living Church*, June 1869, p. 18.

16. "The Public School Question," *Living Church*, Jan. 1870, p. 134.

17. Note in file drawer 18, n.d. See also "Annual Report of the Board of Education, 1888," *Annual Reports of the Board of Education of the State of Connecticut, 1883–1909* (New Haven: State of Connecticut, 1909), p. 11.

18. Apr. 8, 1882, William C. Whitney Correspondence, Historical Manuscripts Division, Library of Congress. See also notes in file drawer 17, n.d.

19. "Population Cont[inued]," [c. 1900], p. 35.

20. Notes in file drawer 9 and 26, n.d.; *The Forgotten Man and Other Essays*, ed. Albert Galloway Keller (New Haven: Yale University Press, 1919), p. 38; "Labor," [c. 1900], n.p.; *Folkways*, pp. 44, 628; "Individuality and Societality," [c. 1900], n.p.

21. "The Strikes," [c. 1880], 20–23; *Earth-Hunger*, p. 10; *Folkways*, pp. 628–29.

22. "The Sphere of Academical Instruction," [c. 1880], n.p.; *War*, p. 175; *Earth-Hunger*, p. 72.

23. Thomas Beer, *The Mauve Decade: American Life at the End of the Nineteenth Century* (Garden City, New York: Garden City Publishing Co., 1926), p. 174.

24. Henry F. Pringle, *The Life and Times of William Howard Taft: A Biography* (New York: Farrar and Rinehart, 1939), p. 34.

25. See Veysey, pp. 14, 28–29; Starr, pp. 373–85; Keller, *Reminiscences*, pp. 3, 8, 24, 27, 29, 68, 86; Ralph Henry Gabriel, *Religion and Learning at Yale: The Church of Christ in the College and University, 1757–1957* (New Haven: Yale University Press, 1958), p. 206; Pierson, pp. 191, 274; *Earth-Hunger*, p. 5.

26. Keller, *Reminiscences*, p.61.

27. May 29, 1874. See also Keller, *Reminiscences*, pp. 58, 100; Letter from M. R. Davie to Keller, July 16, 1926; "Editorial Comment," clipping from unknown newspaper, n.d., n.p.

28. Keller, *Reminiscences*, p. 16.

29. Letter to R. R. Bowker, Dec. 5, n.d., R. R. Bowker Papers, Manuscript Division, New York Public Library.

30. Irwin Unger, *The Greenback Era: A Social and Political History of American Finance, 1865–1879* (Princeton, N.J.: Princeton University Press, 1964), pp. 120–62; John G. Sproat, *The Best Men: Liberal Reformers in the Gilded Age* (New York: Oxford University Press, 1968), passim; Stow Persons, *The Decline of American Gentility* (New York: Columbia University Press, 1973), pp. 131–78; Ari Hoogenboom, *Outlawing the Spoils: A History of the Civil Service Reform Movement, 1865–1883* (Urbana: University of Illinois Press, 1961), passim; David P. Thelen, "Rutherford B. Hayes and the Reform Tradition in the Gilded Age," *American Quarterly*, Summer 1970, pp. 150–65; Richard Hofstadter, *The Age of Reform: From Bryan to F. D. R.* (New York: Vintage, 1960), pp. 135–43; Eric F. Goldman,

*Rendezvous with Destiny: A History of Modern American Reform*, rev. ed. (New York: Vintage Books, 1956), pp. 9, 14–17; Geoffrey T. Blodgett, "The Mind of the Boston Mugwump," *Mississippi Valley Historical Review*, Mar. 1962, pp. 614–34; Gerald W. McFarland, "The New York Mugwumps of 1884: A Profile," *Political Science Quarterly*, Mar. 1963, pp. 40–58; Gordon S. Wood, "The Massachusetts Mugwumps," *New England Quarterly*, Dec. 1960, pp. 435–51.

31. *Protectionism: The -Ism Which Teaches That Waste Makes Wealth* (New York: Henry Holt, 1885), pp. v-vi.

32. Ibid., pp. vi-viii.

33. *Andrew Jackson as a Public Man: What He Was, What Chances He Had, and What He Did with Them*, American Statesmen Series (Boston: Houghton Mifflin, 1883), p. 386.

34. *Alexander Hamilton*, Makers of America Series (New York: Dodd, Mead, 1890), p. iv.

35. *The Financier and the Finances of the American Revolution*, 2 vols. (New York: Dodd, Mead, 1891); *Robert Morris*, Makers of America Series (New York: Dodd, Mead, 1892).

36. *What Social Classes Owe*, p. 12.

37. Ibid., p. 8.

38. *Folkways*, p. 629. See also Robert B. Notestein, "The Moralist Rigorism of W. G. Sumner," *Journal of the History of Ideas*, June 1955, pp. 389–400; Donald K. Pickens, "William Graham Sumner: Moralist as Social Scientist," *Social Science*, Oct. 1968, pp. 202–209.

39. Letter from E. T. Burley, Jan. 28, 1884. See also letter from "Tariff," Feb. 25, 1884; Letter from Charles Bobzin, Feb. 16, 1900.

40. Clipping from *Boston Daily Evening Traveler*, Sept. 28, 1878, n.p.

41. Letter from Thomas Anthony Thatcher to Henry C. Townsend, Sept. 25, 1884. See also Beer, p. 206.

42. Letter to W. C. Ford, Nov. 27, 1882, William Graham Sumner Miscellaneous Manuscripts, New York Public Library.

43. "Sound Talk at Yale," clipping from unknown newspaper, 1876, n.p. See also *Challenge of Facts*, pp. 369–70.

44. *Earth-Hunger*, pp. 4–5.

45. Letter to Keller, July 7, 1906.

46. Untitled [Supply and Demand], [c. 1900], p. 11.

47. Peel, p. 22; Persons, *Gentility*, pp. 284–85.

48. Letter to William C. Whitney, Dec. 1, 1890, William C. Whitney Correspondence, Historical Manuscripts Division, Library of Congress.

49. Letter to William C. Whitney, n.d., William C. Whitney Correspondence, Historical Manuscripts Division, Library of Congress.

50. Letter from William C. Whitney and Others to Sumner, June 20, 1891, William C. Whitney Correspondence, Historical Manuscripts Division, Library of Congress.

51. Letter from Sumner to Eliot Sumner, June 14, 1892; Letter from

Sumner to Jeannie Sumner, June 23, 1893; Letter from Sumner to Edward S. Dana, Aug. 26, 1893.

52. Page Smith, *Daughters of the Promised Land: Women in American History* (Boston: Little, Brown, 1970), pp. 131–39.

53. July 19, 1896. See also William E. Bridges, "Family Patterns and Social Values in America, 1825–1875," *American Quarterly*, Spring 1965, pp. 3–11.

54. Letter from Sumner to Jeannie Elliott, June 6, 1870.

55. Letter from Sumner to Keller, July 7, 1906.

56. Letter from Sumner to Jeannie Sumner, Sat. 12, n.d.; Keller, *Reminiscences,* p. 71; Letter from Sumner to [Norris] Tyler, July 8, 1901; Keller, "Pedagography," 1939, pp. 286–87; Letter from Sumner to [R. R.] Bowker, July 10, 1876.

57. Letter from Keller to Julius C. Peter, Dec. 2, 1948.

58. Letter from Sumner to Keller, n.d.

## Chapter Four

1. *Challenge of Facts*, pp. 398–99.

2. Lecture notes on Political Economy, c. 1874, n.p.

3. *Essays of William Graham Sumner*, ed. Albert Galloway Keller and Maurice R. Davie, Vol. II (New Haven: Yale University Press, 1934), p. 477. Discussions of the classical economists are numerous; see, for example, John Fred Bell, *A History of Economic Thought* (New York: Ronald Press, 1953), pp. 147-396.

4. Note in file drawer 19, n.d.

5. *War*, p. 181.

6. Ibid., p. 182.

7. *Challenge of Facts*, pp. 9–10.

8. Ibid., p. 10. See also "Political Science," [lecture notes], [c. 1874], n.p.; Starr, p. 345.

9. Don Martindale, *The Nature and Types of Sociological Theory* (Boston: Houghton Mifflin, 1960), pp. 186–88; Floyd Nelson House, *The Development of Sociology* (New York: McGraw-Hill, 1936), pp. 173n, 227, 275–76; Keller, "Pedagography," 1939, p. 289; William Graham Sumner and Albert Galloway Keller, *The Science of Society*, Vol. 1. (New Haven: Yale University Press, 1927), pp. xxvii–xxviii; Keller, "Introduction," *War*, pp. xv–xviii; Julius Lippert, *The Evolution of Culture*, trans. George P. Murdock (New York: Macmillan, 1931), pp. xiii–xxiii; Ludwig Gumplowicz, *Outlines of Sociology*, ed. Irving L. Horowitz (New York: Paine-Whitman, 1963), p. 64; Fay Berger Karpf, *American Social Psychology: Its Origins, Development, and European Background* (New York: McGraw-Hill, 1932), p. 74; Albion W. Small, *General Sociology: An Exposition of the Main Development in Sociological Theory from Spencer to Ratzenhofer* (Chicago: University of Chicago, 1905), pp. 332–39.

10. Harald Höffding, *A History of Modern Philosophy: A Sketch of the History of Philosophy from the Close of the Renaissance to Our Own Day,* trans. B. E. Meyer, Vol. 2 (New York: Dover, 1955), pp. 331–32, 336, 345, 470–71; J. D. Y. Peel, *Herbert Spencer: The Evolution of a Sociologist* (New York: Basic Books, 1971), passim; Robert Scoon, "The Rise and Impact of Evolutionary Ideas," in *Evolutionary Thought in America,* ed. Stow Persons (New York: George Braziller, 1956), pp. 12–13, 24–27, 34; Henry F. May, *The End of American Innocence: A Study of the First Years of Our Own Time, 1912–1927* (New York: Knopf, 1959), p. 154; Martindale, pp. 62–65, 74, 189; D. C. Phillips, "Organicism in the Late Nineteenth and Early Twentieth Centuries," *Journal of the History of Ideas,* July-Sept. 1970, pp. 413–32; House, pp. 120, 191, 254, 415; Lewis E. Hill, "On Laissez-faire Capitalism and Liberalism," *American Journal of Economics and Sociology,* Oct. 1964, pp. 393–96; Overton Hume Taylor, "The 'Free Enterprise' Ideology and American Ideals and Institutions," *Daedalus,* Summer 1963, pp. 415–32; Robert C. Bannister, " 'The Survival of the Fittest Is Our Doctrine': History or Histrionics?" *Journal of the History of Ideas,* July-Sept. 1970, pp. 377–98; Cynthia Eagle Russet, *The Concept of Equilibrium in American Social Thought* (New Haven: Yale University Press, 1966), passim; Alfred F. Chalk, "Natural Law and the Rise of Economic Individualism in England," *Journal of Political Economy,* Aug. 1951, pp. 332–47; Merle Curti, "Human Nature in American Thought," *Political Science Quarterly,* Dec. 1953, pp. 493–94.

11. *Forgotten Man,* pp. 404–405.

12. *Challenge of Facts,* p. 208.

13. Ibid., p. 11.

14. "A Private and Personal Communication to the Members of the Corporation and to the Permanent Officers of Yale College," June 1881, n.p.

15. Letter to [Simeon] Baldwin, June 24, 1881.

16. "Science and Mores," n.d., n.p.

17. *Earth-Hunger,* pp. 23–24.

18. *Forgotten Man,* p. 403.

19. *Challenge of Facts,* p. 401.

20. Untitled [Societal Evolution], [c. 1905], p. 26.

21. "Miscellaneous MS no. 1," [c. 1900], p. 10. See also "The Solidarity of the Human Race," 1873, n.p.; *Challenge of Facts,* p. 417; "Mores of the Middle Ages," n.d., p. 8; note in file drawer 18, n.d.; "Political Science" [lecture notes], [c. 1874], n.p.; "Free Trade," [c. 1889], p. 16; *Earth-Hunger,* pp. 70–71.

22. Note in file drawer 19, n.d. See also Lectures on "Social Science," transcribed by Keller, Apr. 14, 1897; Lectures on "Science of Society," transcribed by Bishop, 1902–1903, semester 1, lectures 10 and 28; "Earth-Hunger," 1896, p. 24.

23. "Introduction: Definition and Elementary Principles of Economic

Science," 1878, n.p.; *Forgotten Man,* p. 338; *Challenge of Facts,* p. 411; House, p. 409; notes in file drawers 18, 19, 26, n.d.; *War,* p. 173; "Miscellaneous MS no. 1," [c. 1900], p. 11.

24. *War,* p. 191.

25. "Population 13," [c. 1900], p. 13.

26. *War,* p. 168. See also *Earth-Hunger,* pp. 36–37.

27. *Earth-Hunger,* p. 120. See also note in file drawer 18, n.d.; Untitled [Definition of Societology], [c. 1895], p. 5.

28. Untitled [Supply and Demand], [c. 1900], p. 6; Untitled [Definition of Societology], [c. 1895], pp. 25–26; *Earth-Hunger,* pp. 67–75.

29. Untitled [Definition of Societology], [c. 1895], p. 6. See also *Earth-Hunger,* p. 18; *Challenge of Facts,* p. 410.

30. Lectures on "Science of Society," transcribed by Bishop, 1902–1903, semester 1, lecture 11.

31. Ibid.; note in file drawer 19, n.d.; "Miscellaneous MS no. 1," [c. 1900], p. 10; *Folkways,* pp. 33, 97; *Collected Essays in Political and Social Science* (New York: Henry Holt, 1885), p. 5; *Earth-Hunger,* pp. 358–59; *Challenge of Facts,* p. 399; *What Social Classes Owe,* pp. 119–21; *War,* p. 239; Julius Weinberg, *Edward Alsworth Ross and the Sociology of Progressivism* (Madison: University of Wisconsin Press, 1972), passim; Lester Frank Ward, *Lester Ward and the Welfare State,* ed. Henry Steele Commager (New York: Bobbs-Merrill, 1967), pp. xi-xxxviii and passim.

32. Untitled [Societal Evolution], [c. 1905], p. 29.

33. Harry V. Ball, George E. Simpson, and Kiydshi Ikeda, "Law and Social Change: William Graham Sumner Reconsidered," *American Journal of Sociology,* Mar. 1962, pp. 532–40; "Introduction: Definition and Elementary Principles of Economic Science," 1878, p. 1; Untitled [Supply and Demand], [c. 1900], p. 16; *Folkways,* pp. 117–18; Arthur Bestor, "Patent Office Models of the Good Society," *American Historical Review,* Apr. 1953, p. 523.

34. *What Social Classes Owe,* pp. 59–60; *Challenge of Facts,* pp. 147–48; Lectures on "Mental Reactions," transcribed by Bishop, 1904, p. 34; *Earth-Hunger,* p. 143.

35. *Folkways,* pp. 1–74.

36. Ibid., p. iv.

37. Note in file drawer 18, n.d. See also *Challenge of Facts,* pp. 201–204; *Earth-Hunger,* p. 178; *War,* p. 11; *Folkways,* p. 33.

### Chapter Five

1. " Sociology" [lecture notes], 1896–1902, n.p.

2. *War,* p. 181. See also untitled [Supply and Demand], [c. 1900], p. 34.

3. *Earth-Hunger,* p. 31.

4. *War,* p. 159.

5. *Earth-Hunger*, p. 162. See also "The Strikes," [c. 1880], p. 43.

6. *What Social Classes Owe*, p. 63. See also *Forgotten Man*, pp. 291–92; *Folkways*, p. 39; Edith H. Parker, "William Graham Sumner and the Frontier," *Southwest Review*, Autumn 1956, pp. 357–65.

7. *War*, pp. 174–76; *Forgotten Man*, p. 292; *Challenge of Facts*, pp. 120–21, 155–57; "Socialism," [c. 1878], n.p.; "The Strikes," [c. 1880], p. 43; "Demonism and Witchcraft in the Ancient World," [c. 1904], n.p.; Henry George, *Progress and Poverty: An Inquiry into the Cause of Industrial Depressions and of Increase of Want with Increase of Wealth*, New ed. (New York: Sterling Publishing Co., 1897), passim.

8. Note in file drawer 19, n.d.

9. Note in file drawer 9, n.d.; "Progress," [c. 1900], pp. 2–4.

10. Lectures on "Science of Society," transcribed by Bishop, 1902–1903, semester 1, lecture 18. See also "The Solidarity of the Human Race," 1873, n.p.; Untitled [Definition of Societology], [c. 1895], pp. 13–15; "Individuality and Societality," [c. 1900], n.p.; *War*, p. 272; Note in file drawer 19, n.d.; *Challenge of Facts*, p. 391; "The Ethical Aspects of the Protective System," 1884, n.p.; "Sin," [c. 1902], n.p.

11. *Earth-Hunger*, p. 344; "Relations of Physical to Moral Good," [c. 1873], n.p.; "Syllabus of the Course of Lectures to be Given in Albany by Prof. Sumner on Sociology," 1897, p. 1; note in file drawer 19, n.d.

12. "The Strikes," [c. 1880], p. 13.

13. Note in file drawer 18, n.d. See also note in file drawer 19, n.d.; "Sociology," n.d., pp. 2–3; *Earth-Hunger*, pp. 217–21, 233–38; *Folkways*, p. 16; *War*, pp. 9, 173; "The Lesson of the Panic," [c. 1874], n.p.; "Modern Marriage," [c. 1902], n.p.

14. Sermon no. 73, Mar. 11, 1871.

15. Page 14.

16. *Earth-Hunger*, p. 234. See also *Challenge of Facts*, p. 399; "Have We Had Enough?" [c. 1874], p. 1.

17. *Challenge of Facts*, p. 25. See also *Earth-Hunger*, p. 32; *War*, p. 34.

18. *What Social Classes Owe*, p. 67; *War*, pp. 9, 176; *Earth-Hunger*, pp. 35, 318.

19. "Introduction: Definition and Elementary Principles of Economic Science," 1878, p. 9; Untitled [Societal Evolution], [c. 1905], pp. 1, 58–59; "The Application of the Notions of Evolution and Progress on the Superorganic Domain," 1905, pp. 5–7, 17, 23; "Individuality and Societality," [c. 1900], n.p.; "Good Society," [c. 1900], pp. 1–9; *Folkways*, pp. 16–18.

20. "Introduction: Definition and Elementary Principles of Economic Science," 1878, p. 2; Lectures on "Systematic Sociology," transcribed by Keller, Apr. 12, 1899, p. 16; notes in file drawers 10 and 19, n.d.

21. Lectures on "Science of Society," transcribed by Bishop, 1902–1903, semester 2, lecture 3; Lectures on "Mental Reactions," transcribed by Bishop, 1904, p. 35.

22. Untitled [Definition of Societology], [c. 1895], p. 35. See also note in file drawer 4, n.d.

23. Lectures on "Mental Reactions," transcribed by Bishop, 1904, pp. 31–32.

24. Sermon no. 44, Oct. 21, 1870; Sermon no. 98, Aug. 24, 1871; Lectures on "Science of Society," transcribed by Keller, Dec. 5, 1895; "Societal Organization," [c. 1900], p. 61; *Folkways*, p. 16.

25. Sermon no. 46, Oct. 28, 1870; Note in file drawer 19, n.d.; Lectures on "Social Science," transcribed by Keller; Oct. 28, 1896; Lectures on "Science of Society," transcribed by Bishop, 1902–1903, semester 2, lecture 3; Untitled [Definition of Societology], [c. 1895], p. 35; Untitled [Supply and Demand], [c. 1900], pp. 9–10.

26. Untitled [Definition of Societology], [c. 1895], pp. 9–10, 35; Lectures on "Mental Reactions," transcribed by Bishop, 1904, pp. 31–32; Lectures on "Science of Society," transcribed by Bishop, 1902–1903, semester 1, lecture 8; ibid., semester 2, lecture 15; *Folkways*, pp. 18–19.

27. "Good Society," [c. 1900], p. 4.

28. "Individuality and Societality," [c. 1900], n.p.; Untitled ["Interesse"], [c. 1900], p. 2; notes in file drawers 9 and 19, n.d.

29. Untitled ["Interesse"], [c. 1900], p. 1; notes in file drawers 17, 18, 19, n.d.

30. Lectures on "Systematic Sociology," transcribed by Keller, Apr. 12, 1899, notes in file drawers 10 and 19, n.d.; "Individuality and Societality," [c. 1900], n.p.; Untitled ["Interesse"], [c. 1900], p. 6; "Individuality and Societality," [c. 1900], n.p.

31. Note in file drawer 18, n.d. See also *Earth-Hunger*, p. 347; "Good Society," [c. 1900], pp. 1–9; *War*, pp. 218–19.

32. Sermon no. 11, Feb. 18, 1869.

33. *War*, pp. 8–9, 176; *Folkways*, pp. 16, 164; "The Strikes," [c. 1880], pp. 4–5; "Population Cont[inued]," [c. 1905], p. 1; "The Application of the Notions of Evolution and Progress on the Superorganic Domain," 1905, pp. 3–4; note in file drawer 19, n.d.

34. "Syllabus of the Course of Lectures to be Given in Albany by Prof. Sumner on Sociology," 1895, pp. 1–5; Lectures on "Science of Society," transcribed by Bishop, 1902–1903, semester 1, lecture 13; Note in file drawer 17, n.d.; "Societal Organization,"[c. 1900], p. 48; "Mentality," [c. 1903], p. 42.

35. Richard Hofstadter, *Social Darwinism in American Thought*, rev. ed. (Boston: Beacon Press, 1955), passim; House, pp. 120, 123–24, 158–59; Peel, pp. 92, 99–100, 147–49, 207–209, 234; Martindale, pp. 177, 189; Robert C. Bannister, " 'The Survival of the Fittest Is Our Doctrine': History or Histrionics?" *Journal of the History of Ideas*, July-Sept. 1970, pp. 377–98; R. J. Halliday, "Social Darwinism: A Definition," *Victorian Studies*, June 1971, pp. 389–405; James Allen Rodgers, "Darwinism and Social Darwinism," *Journal of the History of Ideas*, Apr.–June 1972, pp. 265–80.

36. *War*, p. 173.

37. Ibid., p. 177. See also "Individuality and Societality," [c. 1900], n.p.; *Forgotten Man*, p. 404.

38. *Forgotten Man,* p. 225. See also *Challenge of Facts,* pp. 25, 423; Lectures on "Science of Society," transcribed by Bishop, 1902–1903, semester 1, lecture 10.

39. "The Strikes," [c. 1880], p. 18; *War,* p. 185; "The Application of the Notions of Evolution and Progress on the Superorganic Domain," 1905, p. 3; Untitled [Societal Evolution], [c. 1905], pp. 9, 30–32; "Population Cont[inued]," [c. 1905], pp. 30–31; notes in file drawers 18 and 26, n.d.

40. *War,* p. 252.

41. *Challenge of Facts,* p. 29.

42. Notes in file drawers 18 and 26, n.d.; "Money and Its Laws," *International Review,* Jan.-Feb. 1878, p. 77; "Socialism," [c. 1878], n.p.; *Earth-Hunger,* p. 119; "Sociology," n.d., pp. 19–20.

43. *War,* pp. 179, 184–85; *What Social Classes Owe,* pp. 67–68; *Earth-Hunger,* pp. 35–36, 147, 249–51; "Mores," [c. 1900], n.p.; notes in file drawers 17 and 19, n.d; "Individuality and Societality," [c. 1900], n.p.; "Modern Marriage," [c. 1902], n.p.; "Ethical Aspects of the Protective System," 1884, n.p.; *Challenge of Facts,* p. 3.

44. "The Application of the Notions of Evolution and Progress on the Superorganic Domain," 1905, p. 11; notes in file drawers 18 and 26, n.d.; Lectures on "Science of Society," transcribed by Keller, Feb. 24, 1896; ibid., Feb. 26, 1896; *Folkways,* p. 164; note in file drawer 26, n.d.; Untitled [Societal Evolution], [c. 1905], p. 17; *War,* p. 33; "Recent Indications of the Trend of Socialism in the Country," *New York Herald,* Jan. 1, 1906, p. 8.

45. "Ethical Aspects of the Protective System," 1884, n.p. See also untitled notebook, [c. 1893], n.p.

46. "Societal Organization," [c. 1900], pp. 55–56.

47. Page 17.

48. *Folkways,* p. 18.

49. Lectures on "Science of Society," transcribed by Bishop, 1902–1903, semester 1, lecture 1. See also Sermon no. 44, Oct. 21, 1870.

50. Lectures on "Science of Society," transcribed by Bishop, 1902–1903, semester 1, lecture 12. See also untitled notebook [on Spencer's *Principles of Sociology*], [c. 1880], n.p.; note in file drawer 19, n.d.; *War,* p. 174; *What Social Classes Owe,* pp. 67–68; "Societal Organization," [c. 1900], p. 56; *Earth-Hunger,* p. 33; *Folkways,* pp. 2, 18; "Individuality and Societality," [c. 1900], pp. 2–3; *Challenge of Facts,* p. 97; Lectures on "Social Science," transcribed by Keller, Oct. 28, 1896.

51. "Good Society," [c. 1900], p. 1. See also "Syllabus of the Course of Lectues to be Given in Albany by Prof. Sumner on Sociology," 1895, p. 1; Untitled notebook, [c. 1893], n.p.; Sermon no. 44, Oct. 21, 1870; Sermon no. 102, Sept. 9, 1871; Untitled ["Interesse"], [c. 1900], p. 4; Untitled [Societal Evolution], [c. 1905], pp. 5–6.

52. *Forgotten Man,* p. 230. See also *Folkways,* pp. 48–50, 345–46; *War,* pp. 8, 43; note in file drawer 19, n.d.; "Individuality and Societality," [c. 1900], p. 52.

53. Lectures on "Science of Society," transcribed by Bishop, 1902–1903, semester 2, lecture 24. See also lectures on "Finance and the Science and Art of Politics in the History of the United States," transcribed by J. C. Schwab, 1886, p. 29; "Sanctions," 1907, n.p.; notes in file drawers 19 and 28, n.d.

54. *Forgotten Man*, p. 217.

55. "Free Trade," [c. 1889], p. 19; *War*, pp. 7, 178; *What Social Classes Owe*, p. 67; Earth-Hunger, p. 251; notes in file drawers 19 and 26, n.d.; Lectures on "Social Science," transcribed by Keller, Apr. 14, 1897; Lectures on "Mental Outfit," transcribed by Keller, May 25, 1899; "Societal Organization," [c. 1900], p. 48.

56. "Modern Marriage," [c. 1902], pp. 51–55; notes in file drawers 6, 9, 10, n.d.

57. "History," [college class notes], Sept. 1862, lectures 1 and 2.

58. Sermon no. 104, Sept. 16, 1871. See also Sermon no. 17, July 16, 1869.

59. Lectures on "Science of Society," transcribed by Bishop, 1902–1903, semester 2, lecture 24. See also *Folkways*, p. 604; *Challenge of Facts*, pp. 147–50; *War*, p. 241; "Progress," [c. 1900], n.p.

60. *Earth-Hunger*, p. 23; *Folkways*, p. 182.

61. Lectures on "Social Science," transcribed by Keller, Nov. 25, 1896; Lectures on "Science of Society," transcribed by Bishop, 1902–1903; semester 1, lecture 13; Sermon no. 98, Aug. 24, 1871; *What Social Classes Owe*, pp. 71, 75; *Challenge of Facts*, p. 421; "The Application of the Notions of Evolution and Progress on the Superorganic Domain," 1905, p. 13.

62. Untitled [The Glacier], n.d., pp. 1–7.

63. Note in file drawer 18, n.d.

64. "Progress," [c. 1900], n.p. See also *Earth-Hunger*, p. 31; note in file drawer 9, n.d.; Erwin N. Hiebert, "The Uses and Abuses of Thermodynamics in Religion," *Daedalus*, Fall 1966, pp. 1046–80.

65. "The Solidarity of the Human Race," 1873, n.p. See also Untitled [Definition of Societology], [c. 1895], p. 31.

66. Untitled [Definition of Societology], [c. 1895], p. 21.

67. "Progress," [c. 1900], n.p.

### Chapter Six

1. *Folkways*, pp. 40–43.

2. "Propriety," [c. 1903], n.p. See also *Folkways*, pp. 39–40, 42, 45–46, 51; Lectures on "Science of Society," transcribed by Bishop, 1902–1903, semester 2, lecture 35; "A Republican Form of Government," 1877, n.p.; *Earth-Hunger*, pp. 304–305; Untitled [Definition of Societology], [c. 1895], p. 28.

3. "Mores and Science," [c. 1900], n.p.; *Folkways*, pp. 42, 67; Lectures

on "Science of Society," transcribed by Bishop, 1902–1903, semester 2, lectures 35 and 37; *Forgotten Man*, p. 470; *Earth-Hunger*, p. 23; "Operation of Inquisition," [c. 1901], pp. 37–39.

4. *Folkways*, pp. 40–42, 50–53; "Mores," [c. 1900], n.p.

5. Lectures on "History of Finance, Politics, and Political Economy in the United States," transcribed by Raymond S. Bridgman, 1875–76, pp. 1300–1301; *What Social Classes Owe*, pp. 32–33; "Peasants and Land Tenure in Scandinavia," [c. 1889], p. 3; *Challenge of Facts*, p. 69; *War*, pp. 190–91.

6. *Challenge of Facts*, pp. 392–93, 402.

7. "Discussing the Tariff," *New York Times*, Feb. 21, 1885, p. 2.

8. Note in file drawer 9, n.d.; *War*, p. 302; *Essays of William Graham Sumner*, Vol. 1, pp. 227–29; "Mores and Science," [c. 1900], n.p.; *Collected Essays*, p. 103; *Earth-Hunger*, p. 165; Lectures on "Science of Society," transcribed by Keller, Oct. 21, 1896, *Folkways*, pp. 117–18; Lectures on "Political Economy," transcribed by J. C. Schwab, 1886–87, p. 14.

9. Page 53.

10. *New York Tribune*, Feb. 28, 1872, p. 2; *Challenge of Facts*, p. 75; *Earth-Hunger*, p. 315; *Folkways*, p. 53.

11. Lectures on "Science of Society," transcribed by Bishop, 1902–1903, semester 2, lecture 24.

12. "Population Cont[inued]," [c. 1905], p. 32. See also *Folkways*, p. 452.

13. *Earth-Hunger*, pp. 315–16; "Introduction: Definition and Elementary Principles of Economic Science," 1878, pp. 43–44; *Forgotten Man*, p. 228; *Challenge of Facts*, p. 70; William A. Williams, *The Contours of American History* (Cleveland: World Publishing Co., 1961), p. 333.

14. *What Social Classes Owe*, pp. 38–39.

15. *Folkways*, p. 41.

16. Lectures on "History of Finance, Politics, and Political Economy in the United States," transcribed by Bridgman, 1875–76, pp. 517–18. See also *Forgotten Man*, pp. 291–92; *War*, pp. 241–42.

17. "Population 13," [c. 1900], p. 12. See also *War*, pp. 26–27, 241; *Earth-Hunger*, p. 42.

18. *War*, p. 162. See also *Folkways*, p. 376.

19. Lectures on "American History," transcribed by L. M. Daggett, Vol. 1, 1884; n.p.; *Jackson*, p. 136; *Challenge of Facts*, pp. 223, 347; "Introduction: Definition and Elementary Principles of Economic Science," 1878, p. 80.

20. "Democratization of Industry," [c. 1895], n.p.

21. *Forgotten Man*, p. 258. See also "Civil Service Reform," *Chautauquan*, Nov. 1887, p. 78; "Propriety," [c. 1903], n.p.; *Folkways*, pp. 45–56, 51.

22. Sermon no. 108, October 6, 1871.

23. *Essays of William Graham Sumner*, Vol. 1, p. 214.

24. *Forgotten Man*, p. 79.

25. "Introduction: Definition and Elementary Principles of Economic Science," 1878, p. 5.

26. *Forgotten Man*, p. 169.

27. *Earth-Hunger*, p. 70.

28. Charles Albro Barker, *Henry George* (New York: Oxford University Press, 1955), passim.

29. *War*, p. 180.

30. "The Dollar," [c. 1898], n.p.

31. *Challenge of Facts*, p. 165.

32. *Essays of William Graham Sumner*, Vol. 1, p. 230.

33. *Looking Backward, 2000–1887* (Boston: Houghton Mifflin, 1926), p. 326.

34. *War*, p. 205.

35. Ibid., p. 206.

36. Ibid., p. 207.

37. *Forgotten Man*, pp. 166–67, 173.

38. Bruce Curtis, "Sinclair and Sumner: The Private Background of a Public Confrontation," *Mid-America*, Oct. 1978, pp. 185–90.

39. "A Republican Form of Government," 1877, n.p.

40. *Jackson*, p. 97; *Challenge of Facts*, pp. 193–94; *Folkways*, p. 266; "Individuality and Societality," [c. 1900], n.p.

41. *Challenge of Facts*, p. 211.

42. *Essays of William Graham Sumner*, Vol. 1, p. 224.

43. *Forgotten Man*, p. 367. See also *Forgotten Man*, pp. 290–91; *Essays of William Graham Sumner*, Vol. 1, p. 218.

44. *Essays of William Graham Sumner*, Vol. 1, pp. 217–18. See also *Forgotten Man*, pp. 331–32.

45. *Earth-Hunger*, p. 293; *Hamilton*, p. 187; *War*, pp. 159–60.

46. *Challenge of Facts*, p. 224. See also *War*, p. 208; *History of Protection*, p. 12.

47. *Challenge of Facts*, pp. 224, 252–53; *Collected Essays*, pp. 127–30; *What Social Classes Owe*, p. 20.

48. *Challenge of Facts*, p. 253.

49. *Forgotten Man*, p. 332.

50. "Doctrines of Democracy," n.d., n.p.

51. *Folkways*, p. 631.

52. *Hamilton*, p. 14; "Syllabus of American History," n.d., n.p.

53. "Chap[ter] III: American Democracy," n.d., n.p.

54. *Forgotten Man*, p. 331; *Challenge of Facts*, pp. 226–27, 329; *Hamilton*, pp. 142, 242.

55. *Forgotten Man*, pp. 364–65. See also lectures on "American History," transcribed by Daggett, Vol. 1, 1884, n.p.

56. *War*, p. 315. See also *Jackson*, pp. 313, 362.

57. *War*, p. 163. See also *Earth-Hunger*, p. 164.

58. "Civil Service Reform," *Chautauquan*, Nov. 1887, p. 78.

59. Lectures on "History of Finance, Politics and Political Economy in the United States," transcribed by Bridgman, 1875–76, p. 451.

60. *Challenge of Facts*, pp. 335–36.

61. Ibid., p. 344; Letter from Sumner to Jeannie Elliott, June 15, 1870.

62. *Earth-Hunger*, p. 56.

63. Ibid.

64. *Challenge of Facts*, pp. 300–301. See also Höffding, pp. 394–95; Peel, pp. 192–223.

65. *War*, p. 348.

66. Notes in file drawers 17 and 18, n.d.; *War*, pp. 15–16; *Challenge of Facts*, p. 360; *Earth-Hunger*, p. 36; Lectures on "Science of Society," transcribed by Bishop, 1902–1903, semester 1, lecture 19.

67. *Earth-Hunger*, p. 49. See also Lectures on "Science of Society," transcribed by Bishop, 1902–1903, semester 2, lecture 14.

68. Alfred Chalk, "Natural Law and the Rise of Economic Individualism in England," *Journal of Political Economy*, Aug. 1951, pp. 332–47. See also "The Solidarity of the Human Race," 1873, n.p.; Genesis 1:28.

69. *War*, pp. 290–92.

70. Ibid., pp. 297–334.

71. Ibid., p. 302.

72. "The United States as a World Power," clipping from unknown newspaper, 1905.

73. *War*, pp. 303–304.

74. Ibid., pp. 310–11.

75. Ibid., p. 309.

76. Ibid., pp. 325–26.

77. Lectures on "Science of Society," transcribed by Keller, June 2, 1897.

78. Williams, pp. 339–41, 367.

79. *War*, pp. 332–33.

80. Ibid., p. 334.

*Chapter Seven*

1. Lectures on "Science of Society," transcribed by Bishop, 1902–1903, semester 1, lecture 12. See also Untitled [Definition of Societology], [c. 1895], pp. 20–21; *Challenge of Facts*, pp. 391–92; Lectures on "Science of Society," transcribed by Keller, Oct. 31, 1895; Untitled [Supply and Demand], [c. 1900], pp. 32–33.

2. *War*, pp. 8, 13, 348; "Sociology" [The Predicament of Sociological Study], [c. 1900], pp. 2–4; note in file drawer 17, n.d.; "Unrestricted Commerce," *Chautauquan*, June 1887, n.p.; "Syllabus of the Course of Lectures to Be Given in Albany by Prof. Sumner on Sociology," 1897, p. 3;

*Essays of William Graham Sumner,* Vol. 1, pp. 213–14; *Challenge of Facts,* pp. 85–86; Lectures on "Science of Society," transcribed by Bishop, 1902–1903, semester 1, lecture 18.

3. Notes in file drawer 17, n.d.

4. "Land," [c. 1900], p. 40.

5. Ibid.; notes in file drawer 19, n.d.; "The Strikes," [c. 1880], p. 8; *What Social Classes Owe,* pp. 63–64; Lectures on "Political Economy," transcribed by J. C. Schwab, 1886, p. 1; Lectures on "Science of Society," transcribed by Keller, Feb. 3, 1896; *Essays of William Graham Sumner,* Vol. 1, p. 211; *Earth-Hunger,* pp. 20–21; "Syllabus of the Course of Lectures to Be Given in Albany by Prof. Sumner on Sociology," 1897, p. 3.

6. *War,* p. 257. See also Lectures on "Political Economy," transcribed by Schwab, 1886, p. 8; notes from file drawers 18, 19, and 28, n.d.; "Peasants and Land Tenure in Scandinavia," [c. 1889], p. 3; *Forgotten Man,* p. 228; *What Social Classes Owe,* p. 66; *Essays of William Graham Sumner,* Vol. 1, pp. 232–33; Lectures on "Science of Society," transcribed by Bishop, 1902–1903, semester 1, lecture 18.

7. *What Social Classes Owe,* p. 66.

8. *Challenge of Facts,* p. 392.

9. *Earth-Hunger,* p. 284.

10. *What Social Classes Owe,* p. 85; *Essays in Political and Social Science,* p. 56; *History of Protection,* pp. 23, 52; "Political Economy" [lecture notes], [c. 1874], n.p.; *Challenge of Facts,* pp. 97–98, 119, 170–74; *Jackson,* p. 187; *Forgotten Man,* pp. 70–72; *Earth-Hunger,* pp. 38–39, 193–96, 296–97; Lectures on "History of Finance, Politics and Political Economy in the United States," transcribed by Raymond S. Bridgman, 1875–76, p. 972.

11. "Relation of Physical to Moral Good," [c. 1873], n.p.; *Challenge of Facts,* p. 35; "An Eight-Hour Day," *Popular Science News,* June 1888, p. 83; *War,* pp. 234–36, 239–43, 250–51; "Regulation of Contracts," *Science,* Mar. 5, 1886, pp. 227–28; *Earth-Hunger,* pp. 286–87; *Forgotten Man,* p. 246.

12. "Introduction: Definitions and Elementary Principles of Economic Science," 1878, pp. 46, 81–82. See also "The Strikes," [c. 1880], p. 11; *What Social Classes Owe,* pp. 89–90; *War,* pp. 250–52.

13. "The Relation of Political Economy to the Labor Question," Unsigned editorial, *Nation,* Aug. 31, 1882, p. 184.

14. *Challenge of Facts,* p. 102; *Essays in Political and Economic Science,* p. 56; *Forgotten Man,* pp. 243, 251–52; *What Social Classes Owe,* pp. 89–90; *Challenge of Facts,* pp. 99–100.

15. *What Social Classes Owe,* pp. 89–90. See also "Introduction: Definitions and Elementary Principles of Economic Science," 1878, p. 84.

16. *Forgotten Man,* p. 262.

17. Ibid.

18. Lectures on "Politics and Finance in the History of the United

States," transcribed by Horatio M. Reynolds, 1880–81, n.p.; *Challenge of Facts*, p. 58; note in file drawer 28, n.d.

19. Untitled [Societal Evolution], [c. 1905], p. 10; *Folkways*, pp. 162–63; *Earth-Hunger*, pp. 131, 134, 252–53; *Challenge of Facts*, pp. 89–90, 173; "Individuality and Societality," [c. 1900], n.p.

20. "Advancing Social and Political Organization in the United States," [c. 1896], n.p. Cf. *Challenge of Facts*, pp. 289–344.

21. *What Social Classes Owe*, pp. 54–55; *Earth-Hunger*, pp. 67–75.

22. Sermon no. 33, Aug. 25, 1870.

23. "Relation of Physical to Moral Good," [c. 1873], n.p.

24. *Earth-Hunger*, p. 298; *Jackson*, pp. 225–26.

25. "Introduction: Definition and Elementary Principles of Economic Science," 1878, p. 80; Lectures on "American History," transcribed by Daggett, Vol. 3, 1884; n.p.; *War*, pp. 202–203.

26. Letter to Mr. Frost, Mar. 6, 1898, in Keller, *Reminiscences*, pp. 74–75. See also *Forgotten Man*, p. 79; *Jackson*, pp. 225–26; Lectures on "American History," transcribed by Daggett, Vol. 3, 1884, n.p.; *Essays of William Graham Sumner*, Vol. 1, p. 220; *Earth-Hunger*, p. 288; *War*, pp. 56–60; "The Strikes," [c. 1880], n.p.; *History of Protection*, p. 62; "Prof. Sumner's Views Respecting the Tariff Question," *New Haven Register*, Oct. 12, 1880, n.p.; *Challenge of Facts*, p. 271.

27. *Earth-Hunger*, pp. 329–30.

28. "Recent Indications of the Trend of Socialism in the Country," *New York Herald*, Jan. 1, 1906, p. 8.

29. *Forgotten Man*, pp. 136–37.

30. *War*, p. 160.

31. *Earth-Hunger*, pp. 135, 242–49; *Forgotten Man*, p. 257.

32. *Collected Essays*, pp. 16–17; *Earth-Hunger*, pp. 310–11.

33. *What Social Classes Owe*, pp. 140–41.

34. *Folkways*, p. 17. See also *War*, p. 8; "The Good Society," [c. 1900], pp. 1–9; Untitled [Societal Evolution], [c. 1905], p. 20.

35. *Challenge of Facts*, p. 82.

36. "Syllabus of Six Lectures," Jan.-Feb. 1898, p. 6; Lectures on "Science of Society," transcribed by Bishop, 1902–1903, semester 1, lecture 18; *Forgotten Man*, pp. 259, 262; Louis Filler, *Crusaders for American Liberalism*, new ed. (Yellow Springs, Ohio: Antioch Press, 1950), p. 327; Lectures on "Science of Society," transcribed by Keller, Jan. 30, 1896; *Earth-Hunger*, p. 253; "Article I. The Economics of Trusts," *Journal of Commerce and Commercial Bulletin*, June 24, 1901, p. 4; "Article II. Policy in Regard to Trusts," *Journal of Commerce and Commercial Bulletin*, June 25, 1901, p. 4.

37. U. S. Congress, House Select Committee, *Investigation Relative to the Causes of Depression*, 45th Cong., 3d Sess., 1878, House Misc. Doc. 29, p. 208.

38. Page 110. See also pp. 47, 109.

39. *Challenge of Facts*, pp. 182, 218; *Earth-Hunger*, pp. 277–78.

40. *Essays of William Graham Sumner*, Vol. 2, p. 475.

41. *History of Protection*, p. 47.

42. *Earth-Hunger*, p. 324. See also *Challenge of Facts*, p. 318.

43. *Earth-Hunger*, pp. 306–11; "Some Words on Financial Crisis," [c. 1900], pp. 3–4; "Article II. Policy in Regard to Trusts," *Journal of Commerce and Commercial Bulletin*, June 25, 1901, p. 4.

44. *Challenge of Facts*, p. 84.

45. *Earth-Hunger*, p. 314; *War*, p. 205; *Jackson*, p. 226; *Challenge of Facts*, p. 207.

46. "Indiscreet Denunciation and Laws," *Everybody's Magazine*, Dec. 1907, pp. 832b–832c. See also *Challenge of Facts*, p. 182; *Earth-Hunger*, p. 329.

47. Stow Persons, *American Minds: A History of Ideas* (New York: Henry Holt, 1958), p. 228; *Challenge of Facts*, p. 173; *Earth-Hunger*, pp. 144–45, 250; "Syllabus of Six Lectures," Jan.-Feb. 1898, p. 6; Lectures on "Science of Society," transcribed by Bishop, 1902–1903, semester 1, lecture 18.

48. See Bruce Curtis, "William Graham Sumner 'On the Concentration of Wealth,'" *Journal of American History*, Mar. 1969, pp. 823–32. Albert Galloway Keller, Sumner's editor, made headnotes describing the essay's contents and apparently titled it after his assistant, Maurice R. Davie, brought the typescript essay to his attention. Why Keller chose not to publish the essay is uncertain. Certainly, at first glance, it would not have appeared to be consistent with Sumner's social and political attitudes, as Keller understood them. As preceding discussion has indicated, however, the essay is consonant with Sumner's developing views in his later years about the danger of monopolies and about the need for government to regulate them.

49. "On the Concentration of Wealth," [c. 1909], p. 1.

50. Ibid., p. 2. Cf. Ray Stannard Baker, "What the United States Steel Corporation Really Is and How It Works," *McClure's* 18 (1901): 6, in H. Wayne Morgan, ed., *The Gilded Age: A Reappraisal* (Syracuse, N.Y.: Syracuse University Press, 1963), p. 16; Woodrow Wilson, *The New Freedom: A Call for the Emancipation of the Generous Energies of a People* (New York: Doubleday, Page, 1918), p. 6.

51. Filler, p. xiv; John Chamberlain, *Farewell to Reform: Being a History of the Rise, Life and Decay of the Progressive Mind in America* (New York: Liveright, 1932), p. 16; David Mark Chalmers, *The Social and Political Ideas of the Muckrakers* (New York: Citadel Press, 1964), pp. 107–12.

52. "On the Concentration of Wealth," [c. 1909], pp. 2–3.

53. Hofstadter, *Age of Reform*, p. 173.

54. "On the Concentration of Wealth," [c. 1909], p. 3; cf. Wilson, p. 286.

55. *Earth-Hunger*, pp. 322–23.

56. *What Social Classes Owe*, pp. 30–32; "Progress," [c. 1900], p. 1; *Essays of William Graham Sumner*, Vol. 1, p. 212; *Folkways*, p. 169; *Hamilton*, p. 184; *War*, pp. 190–91, 222–23, 316–17; "A Republican Form of Government," 1877, n.p.; *Forgotten Man*, pp. 232, 258.

57. *Forgotten Man*, p. 350. See also "President on Civil Liberty" [college class notes], 1863, lectures 2, 5, 6, 8; Lectures on "History of Finance, Politics and Political Economy in the United States," transcribed by Bridgman, 1875–76, pp. 1300–1301; *Challenge of Facts*, pp. 238–39, 261; *Collected Essays*, p. 99; *What Social Classes Owe*, p. 41; *Earth-Hunger*, p. 364; "Progress," [c. 1900], p. 9; *War*, p. 235.

58. *War*, pp. 219.

59. *Earth-Hunger*, pp. 306–307.

60. *What Social Classes Owe*, p. 9; See Chamberlain, pp. 12–15; Robert G. McCloskey, *American Conservatism in the Age of Enterprise: A Study of William Graham Sumner, Stephen J. Field, and Andrew Carnegie* (Cambridge, Mass.: Harvard University Press, 1951), pp. 61–62.

61. Ralph Henry Gabriel, *The Course of American Democratic Thought*, 2nd ed. (New York: Ronald Press, 1956), p. 360; Peter G. Filene, "An Obituary for 'The Progressive Movement,'" *American Quarterly*, Spring 1970, pp. 20–34; J. Joseph Huthmacher, "Urban Liberalism in the Age of Reform," *Mississippi Valley Historical Review*, Sept. 1962, pp. 231–41; Samuel P. Hays, *The Response to Industrialism, 1885–1914* (Chicago: University of Chicago Press, 1957), pp. 23, 140–43, 152–55; Hofstadter, *Age of Reform*, passim; George E. Mowry, *The Era of Theodore Roosevelt: 1900–1912* (New York: Harper and Row, 1958), passim; Henry F. May, *The End of American Innocence: A Study of the First Years of Our Time, 1912–1917* (New York: Knopf, 1959), pp. 21–23; Arthur P. Dudden, "Nostalgia and the American," *Journal of the History of Ideas*, Oct.-Dec. 1961, pp. 515–30; Robert H. Wiebe, *Businessmen and Reform: A Study of the Progressive Movement* (Chicago: Quadrangle Books, 1962), pp. 6–7, 211–12; Arthur P. Dudden, "Men Against Monopoly: The Prelude to Trust-Busting," *Journal of the History of Ideas*, Oct. 1957, pp. 587–93; Sidney Fine, *Laissez Faire and the General-Welfare State: A Study of Conflict in American Thought, 1865–1901* (Ann Arbor: University of Michigan Press, 1956), passim; Charles Forcey, *The Crossroads of Liberalism* (New York: Oxford University Press, 1961), pp. xx–xxiv; Allen J. Matusow, "The Mind of B. O. Flower," *New England Quarterly*, Dec. 1961, pp. 492–509; Sidney Fine, "Richard T. Ely, Forerunner of Progressivism," *Mississippi Valley Historical Review*, Mar. 1951, pp. 599–624; Arthur Mann, "Frank Parsons: The Professor as Crusader," *Mississippi Valley Historical Review*, Dec. 1950, pp. 471–90; David Chalmers, "Ray Stannard Baker's Search for Reform," *Journal of the History of Ideas*, June 1958, pp. 422–34.

62. Theodore Roosevelt, *The New Nationalism* (New York: The Outlook Company, 1911), pp. 15–18 and passim; Wilson, passim.

63. *What Social Classes Owe*, p. 101.

## Chapter Eight

1. Hofstadter, *Social Darwinism*, pp. 51–66; McCloskey, pp. 22–71; *Social Darwinism: Selected Essays of William Graham Sumner*, ed. Stow Persons (Englewood Cliffs, N.J.: Prentice-Hall, 1963); Persons, *American Minds*, pp. 244–50; Gabriel, pp. 227–41.

2. Notes in file drawers 19 and 32, n.d.; Untitled [Societal Evolution], [c. 1905], p. 19.

3. Keller, *Reminiscences*, p. 109. Cf. Persons, *American Minds*, pp. 222, 230; Frederic Cople Jaher, *Doubters and Dissenters: Cataclysmic Thought in America, 1885–1918* (London: Free Press of Glencoe, 1964), passim.

# Selected Bibliography

PRIMARY SOURCES

*The Forgotten Man and Other Essays*, ed. Albert Galloway Keller (New Haven: Yale University Press, 1919), contains an extensive bibliography of Sumner's publications, which is slightly expanded in volume two of *Essays of William Graham Sumner*, 2 vols., ed. Albert Galloway Keller and Maurice R. Davie (New Haven: Yale University Press, 1934). Since most of Sumner's published works appear there, a complete listing of publications here would be redundant; but I have listed Sumner's books and a number of his more important published articles. For a more complete view of Sumner's thought, however, the investigator should examine the extensive collection of Sumner papers in Historical Manuscripts and Archives of Yale University, in Yale's Beinecke Rare Book and Manuscripts Library, and in the manuscript repositories of the other institutions which I thank in the Preface. For guidance to unpublished material concerning various areas of Sumner's thought, readers may examine the preceding Notes and References.

## 1. Books

*Alexander Hamilton*. Makers of America Series. New York: Dodd, Mead, and Co., 1890.

*Andrew Jackson as a Public Man: What He Was, What Chances He Had, and What He Did with Them*. American Statesmen Series. Boston: Houghton, Mifflin and Co., 1883.

*The Books of the Kings*, by K. C. W. F. Bähr. Book 2, trans. William Graham Sumner. New York: Scribner, Armstrong and Co., 1872.

*The Challenge of Facts and Other Essays*. Ed. Albert Galloway Keller. New Haven: Yale University Press, 1914.

*Collected Essays in Political and Social Science*. New York: Henry Holt, 1885.

*Earth-Hunger and Other Essays*. Ed. Albert Galloway Keller. New Haven: Yale University Press, 1913.

*Essays of William Graham Sumner*. 2 vols. Ed. Albert Galloway Keller and Maurice R. Davie. New Haven: Yale University Press, 1934.

*The Financier and the Finances of the American Revolution.* 2 vols. New York: Dodd, Mead, and Co., 1891.

*Folkways: A Study of the Sociological Importance of Usages, Manners, Customs, Mores, and Morals.* 1906; rpt. New York: Dover Publications, 1959.

*The Forgotten Man and Other Essays.* Ed. Albert Galloway Keller. New Haven: Yale University Press, 1919.

*A History of American Currency.* New York: Henry Holt, 1874.

*History of Banking in the United States.* New York: The Journal of Commerce and Commercial Bulletin, 1896.

*Lectures on the History of Protection in the United States.* New York: Putnam's, 1888.

*Protectionism: The -Ism Which Teaches That Waste Makes Wealth.* New York: Henry Holt, 1885.

*Robert Morris.* Makers of America Series. New York: Dodd, Mead, and Co., 1892.

*War and Other Essays.* Ed. Albert Galloway Keller. New Haven: Yale University Press, 1911.

*What Social Classes Owe to Each Other.* New York: Harper and Brothers, 1883.

Sumner, William Graham and Keller, Albert Galloway. *The Science of Society.* 4 vols. New Haven: Yale University Press, 1927.

## 2. Articles

Since the following articles have been reprinted in the four volumes of Sumner essays, I have included the original date of publication of each article and the volume in which it was reprinted. Complete original publication information may be found in the bibliography of *The Forgotten Man and Other Essays.*

"The Absurd Effort to Make the World Over" (1894), *War,* 195–210.

"Advancing Social and Political Organization in the United States" (1896 or 1897), *Challenge of Facts,* 289–344.

"The Challenge of Facts" (1880s), *Challenge of Facts,* 17–52.

"The Concentration of Wealth: Its Economic Justification" (1902), *Challenge of Facts,* 81–90.

"The Conquest of the United States by Spain" (1899), *War,* 297–334.

"Democracy and Plutocracy" (1888), *Earth-Hunger,* 283–89.

"Democracy and Responsible Government" (1877), *Challenge of Facts,* 243–86.

"Earth Hunger or the Philosophy of Land Grabbing" (1896), *Earth-Hunger,* 31–64.

"The Family and Social Change" (1909), *War,* 43–61.

"Industrial War" (1886), *Challenge of Facts,* 93–102.

"Integrity in Education" (1880s?), *Forgotten Man,* 409–19.

"Liberty and Machinery" (1890), *Earth-Hunger,* 193–98.

"The Mores of the Present and the Future" (1909), *War*, 149–64.
"Power and Progress" (1891), *Challenge of Facts*, 145–50.
"The Science of Sociology" (1883), *Forgotten Man*, 401–405.
"The Scientific Attitude of Mind" (1905), *Earth-Hunger*, 17–28.
"Separation of State and Market" (1889), *Earth-Hunger*, 306–11.
"Sociology" (1881), *War*, 167–92.
"Trusts and Trades-Unions" (1888), *Forgotten Man*, 257–62.
"War" (1903), *War*, 3–40.
"What Makes the Rich Richer and the Poor Poorer?" (1887), *Challenge of Facts*, 65–77.

### SECONDARY SOURCES

ARMENTANO, DOMINICK T. "The Political Economy of William Graham Sumner." Ph.D. dissertation. University of Connecticut, 1967. Examines Sumner's economic views in their nineteenth-century context.

BALL, HARRY V.; SIMPSON, GEORGE E.; AND IKEDA, KIYOSHI. "Law and Social Change: William Graham Sumner Reconsidered." *American Journal of Sociology*, Mar. 1962, pp. 532–40. Details Sumner's recognition that positive law can contribute to social changes.

BANNISTER, ROBERT C., JR. "William Graham Sumner's Social Darwinism: A Reconsideration." *History of Political Economy*, Spring 1973, pp. 89–109. Analyses of Sumner as a "social Darwinist" have been excessively broad and inexact and have slighted other aspects of his changing ideas.

CHAMBERLAIN, JOHN. *Farewell to Reform: Being a History of the Rise, Life and Decay of the Progressive Mind in America.* New York: Liveright, Inc., 1932. Contains an insightful discussion of Sumner as a libertarian, especially of his defective view of the state.

CURTIS, BRUCE. "The Middle Class Progressivism of William Graham Sumner." Ph.D. dissertation. University of Iowa, 1964. Examines a wide range of Sumner's ideas in attempting to explain why he ultimately turned toward government regulation of monopolies.

———. "Sinclair and Sumner: The Private Background of a Public Confrontation." *Mid-America*, Oct. 1978, pp. 185–90. Examines the background of a controversy over Socialism in articles that Sumner and Upton Sinclair wrote for *Collier's Weekly*, a controversy which the editors fomented and managed.

———. "Victorians Abed: William Graham Sumner on the Family, Women, and Sex." *American Studies*, Spring 1977, pp. 101–22. Argues that this case study of Sumner's views about sexual roles questions the assumption of Victorian consensus about sexuality and suggests that further investigation of the views of individuals will reveal that "complex adjustment was truly the mode."

———. "William Graham Sumner and the Problem of Progress." *New*

*England Quarterly*, Sept. 1978, pp. 348–69. Shows that Sumner vacillated in his views about the nature and varieties of progress but tended to come to pessimistic conclusions about the human prospect.

————. "William Graham Sumner 'On the Concentration of Wealth.'" *Journal of American History*, Mar. 1969, pp. 823–32. Presents Sumner's unpublished essay "On the Concentration of Wealth" and places it in the context of his thought.

FINE, SIDNEY. *Laissez Faire and the General-Welfare State: A Study of Conflict in American Thought, 1861–1901.* Ann Arbor: University of Michigan Press, 1956. Offers useful summaries of conservative and reformist ideologies and places Sumner in perspective.

GABRIEL, RALPH HENRY. *The Course of American Democratic Thought.* 2nd ed. New York: Ronald Press, 1956. Emphasizes Sumner's laissez-faire individualism, but cogently discusses his scientism and social Darwinism as well.

HOFSTADTER, RICHARD. *Social Darwinism in American Thought.* Rev. ed. Boston: Beacon Press, 1955. Stresses Sumner's social Darwinism to the virtual exclusion of other aspects of his thought.

HOUSE, FLOYD NELSON. *The Development of Sociology.* New York: McGraw-Hill, 1936. Includes a sound discussion of the sources and characteristics of Sumner's sociology.

KAUFFELD, FREDERICK J. "A Burkean Analysis of Selected Speeches of William Graham Sumner." M.A. thesis. University of Kansas, 1965. Analyzes Sumner's system of argumentation and the values it expresses.

KELLER, ALBERT GALLOWAY. *Reminiscences (Mainly Personal) of William Graham Sumner.* New Haven: Yale University Press, 1933. A storehouse of admiring memories.

MCCLOSKEY, ROBERT G. *American Conservatism in the Age of Enterprise: A Study of William Graham Sumner, Stephen J. Field and Andrew Carnegie.* Cambridge, Mass.: Harvard University Press, 1951. Views Sumner as an unimaginative materialist, a social Darwinist spokesman for big business.

MARTINDALE, DON. *The Nature and Types of Sociological Theory.* Boston: Houghton Mifflin, 1960. Useful for understanding Sumner's ideas in the context of the development of sociology.

NOTESTEIN, ROBERT BRUCE, JR. "The Moralist Rigorism of William Graham Sumner." *Journal of the History of Ideas*, June 1955, pp. 389–400. Summarizes Sumner's ideas and attitudes, especially moralism and social Darwinism.

————. "William Graham Sumner." Ph.D. dissertation. University of Wisconsin, 1954. Finds Sumner's "value orientation" in "intra-worldly asceticism" deriving from middle-class orientation and desire to rise in society.

————. "William Graham Sumner: An Essay in the Sociology of Knowledge." *American Journal of Economics and Sociology*, July 1959, pp.

397–413. Undertakes a psychobiographical understanding of Sumner in light of his mother's death, his shrewish stepmother, and his undemonstrative father.

PAGE, CHARLES H. *Class and American Sociology.* New York: Schocken, 1940. Soundly analyzes Sumner's class views and attitudes.

PARKER, EDITH H. "William Graham Sumner and the Frontier." *Southwest Review,* Autumn 1956, pp. 357–65. Calls attention to Sumner's views of the frontier that anticipated those of Frederick Jackson Turner.

PEEL, J. D. Y. *Herbert Spencer: The Evolution of a Sociologist.* New York: Basic Books, 1971. A detailed discussion of Spencer and his intellectual and social milieu.

PERSONS, STOW. *American Minds: A History of Ideas.* New York: Henry Holt, 1958. Carefully examines Sumner's outlook in the perspective of late-nineteenth-century Naturalism. Especially important in discussing "antagonistic cooperation."

———. *Social Darwinism: Selected Essays of William Graham Sumner.* Englewood Cliffs, N.J.: Prentice-Hall, 1963. Includes an instructive introduction to several essays from Sumner's "middle" period.

PICKENS, DONALD K. "William Graham Sumner (1840–1910) and Scottish Moral Philosophers of the Eighteenth Century: The Missing Link." *Proceedings of the Fall Sociological Research Symposium, East Texas State University,* Oct. 15, 1977, pp. 27–39. The impress of Sumner's training in Scottish moral philosophy was more important for his thought than was his later "social Darwinism."

———. "William Graham Sumner: Moralist as Social Scientist." *Social Science,* Oct. 1968, pp. 202–209. Links Sumner to Scottish moral philosophy.

SHEKETOFF, MERWIN. "William Graham Sumner: Social Christian, 1869–1872." Ph.D. Dissertation. Harvard University, 1961. Argues that Sumner was a pioneer in the social-gospel movement.

STARR, HARRIS E. *William Graham Sumner.* New York: Henry Holt, 1925. Provides much information unavailable elsewhere.

# Index

183